Prospecting for Old Furniture

Prospecting for Old Furniture

Your Guide to Buying and Restoring
Affordable Antiques for Your Home

Don Marotta

Illustrations by Debra L. Sheffer

Stackpole Books

Library of Congress Cataloging in Publication Data

Marotta, Don.
    Prospecting for old furniture.

    Includes index.
    1. Furniture—Collectors and collecting.
2. Furniture finishing.   3. Furniture—Repairing.
I. Title.
NK2240.M375   1985   749'.1'0750973   85-7937
ISBN 0-8117-2178-7

Contents

1

The Old Furniture Boom

The old furniture discussed in this book is for home use and enjoyment. Most people do more with their furniture than simply admire it from behind a velvet rope. For them, aesthetics is significant, but not to the exclusion of practical matters.

Since about 1970, many shoppers have turned to old furniture because much of it combines beauty and usefulness with reasonable prices. Even if today's prices are higher, there are still, at least, the benefits of nondepreciation and a potential profit to be made if resale becomes a necessity. Although old furniture's favorable economics alone motivates many people to investigate it, once they've done so they find that it exists in a wide variety and with enough quality and charm to overcome negative stereotypes. After gaining some familiarity with old furniture, they seldom see it as cheap, tacky, or second-class, and many become old furniture romantics.

Defining Old Furniture

People have come to use the phrase *old furniture* with different connotations and dates. In this book, the old furniture label will be used for articles that are chronologically between expensive *period* furniture (art furniture generally made before 1830), and *used* furniture, the worn and traded items made within the past thirty or forty years or so.

The dates for old furniture, 1830–1945, are somewhat arbitrary and are intended to give the approximate scope of the book. No doubt there are some items in the old furniture category that were made before 1830 and have survived and can be bought reasonably. Similarly there are some made after that date that deserve to be called antiques. Of the furniture made since 1945, a date that represents nothing except perhaps a fuller burgeoning of modern furniture at the end of World War II, many items are being sought as at least classic if not antique. In popular usage the meaning of the term *antique* has expanded in recent years. Because of an increased interest, an antique is now considered anything in demand that is no longer being produced.

Different Styles

The styles of old furniture are distinctly different from those of today's items. Many articles, especially those made before 1910, have much more decoration and detail. All sorts of ornamentation was used, several types of carving and grooving and a vast number of added-on parts. Decorative hardware was a feature of several styles. In most old furniture a primary ingredient was a prominent display of wood texture and color. On the other hand, some of the styles, especially country furniture, are popular with us now because their designs are very simple.

Because old furniture *is* old, it varies greatly in its condition. Many pieces can be restored reasonably and provide some savings plus a worthwhile challenge. Sometimes, though, the savings are too small and the challenge too formidable. Several pages in later chapters will deal with recognizing the difference before you buy.

The Old Furniture Market

Although old furniture has had previous periods of popularity, the interest in it during the last several years is unprecedented. Not only has the demand increased, but efforts to meet the demand have reached into the contents of almost every idle attic, basement, and outbuilding. A large uncovered supply of old furniture

has enabled antique shops and flea markets to pop up almost wherever there is a vacant building. Where supplies have been great, old furniture has been bought up and shipped to relatively lean places like Florida, Texas, and California. Prices have gone from dirt cheap to inexpensive to almost competitive with new furniture. A recent increase in prices is almost entirely due to inflation.

The Antiques Boom

The demand for old furniture has been a leading part of a general antiques boom. Practically anything old and in some sense stylish has become popular. Attractive, useful things like glassware, linens, and china have been in very wide demand, while purely decorative things like jewelry, lace, and ornamental ceramics have fared almost as well. The latest trend has been a great popularity of all things collectible. Many different items, ranging from railroad lanterns to bottle openers to snuff boxes, have been bought up quickly. Old furniture, although generally not collectible or sought after purely for its decorative qualities, has had a large share in the boom because, by and large, it is something that is needed.

Old vs. New

Actually old furniture has come into demand for a great complex of reasons, most of which boil down to the fact that it is a better buy, in almost every way, than new furniture. To begin with, old furniture was made of natural wood rather than the simulated materials used in many current articles. Even compared with today's real wood factory products, old furniture was usually made from better timbers having prettier grain and was usually constructed of solid wood rather than veneer. Even when veneer was used it was in thicker proportions than the frequent standard of $\frac{1}{28}$ inch used at present (veneer thickness did decline beginning in the thirties but was not a widespread fact as it is today).

Although some of today's simulated materials are practical in many circumstances, many people object to them on grounds of inauthenticity. Most of them are some form of plastic used in conjunction with a core of pressed wood chips. It is not uncommon for an article of new furniture to have two, three, or more kinds of plastic involved in its production. Formica, vinyl-clad chipboard, and molded styrene can all be found in the same item. Some of the broader surfaces of new furniture ironically are photographs of real wood developed onto plastic.

Another recent trend is the use of factory-simulated age marks. Many factories, even the ones using fine woods and construction methods, have developed the art of the worm hole, the fly speck, and pieces of spider web. In place of an earlier use of hand-wielded chains and hatchets, special embossing machines have been developed that roll distress marks into wood. A great deal of new furniture strives to look old.

A Factor of Nondepreciation

While the old furniture boom is partly a result of a desire for more genuine materials and better taste in general, it also is largely a matter of economics. For a long time old furniture was a hedge against inflation and a closet bargain many people were discovering for themselves. Today, as demand is exceeding supply, it is less of a bargain, but still makes much better pocketbook sense than new furniture. New furniture is notorious for declining almost 50 percent in its first two years, much of it immediately. Old furniture has age to begin with, the signs of which, if they are not too extreme, are often considered desirable. New furniture wear is generally perceived as tainting.

Today's old furniture trend of mass popularity originated and gained strength largely because of a recognition of its better woods and construction. With increased appeal, old furniture began to rise above the status of used furniture (the two had generally been perceived as the same before the boom). An increased demand, while it sent prices up, also created an investment level of nondepreciation and often a profit for items placed back on the market. Because we were in a period of rampant inflation, with old furniture one of the rare consumer goods with at least a break-even investment value, the news of old furniture quickly spread and has persisted over a longer period than would be expected from mere fad activity.

Its investment status, while it has lessened some, is still at a high level with plenty of evidence that it will continue. It is highly probable that old furniture has reached the point at which, it has become a permanent alternative to new furniture with many, many people. For more information on investment and resale see the first section of chapter 9.

Practical Aesthetics

Old Furniture Charm

Many people who like *antiques* (this popular term, often applied to old furniture, will be used in its place occasionally) like them largely for their charm. There are probably a dozen or more facets of old furniture charm, but some of the foremost are the prominent decorations, softer luster, and quaint and more interesting appearance. The design and hardware of antiques make them a special contrast to contemporary furniture.

Refinishing It Yourself

Other reasons for the great popularity of old furniture are the pleasure and savings many people derive from restoring things they buy "in the rough." People whose jobs involve them in abstraction and uncertainty often find a significant satisfaction in working with their hands and conquering a part of the concrete world of the mechanical. Most people who refinish also enjoy the relaxation of working at their own pace.

Old furniture, in addition to the several advantages noted, is also very relaxing to live with. Not only is it not spoiled by an occasional scratch or dent, but it creates a feeling of ease through its natural grain, warm colors, and soft luster. Through these features it can impart an almost unequaled comfort to a room.

Other Facets

While old furniture offers many different things, new items usually make their appeal through being fashionable or innovative. "The latest thing" idea has probably sold more furniture than any influence except the customers' practical need for it. A changing fashion is part of the life support system of the new furniture industry. It is such an integral part of things that even industry concerns for quality have to compete with it and are at a disadvantage because fashion can usually be sold for considerably less than quality.

Many people have just a casual interest in old furniture. Some of them see it only as something used, dirty, out of date, and decidedly a backward step in terms of personal advancement. On the other side of the fence, many of those who prefer old furniture perceive it as fashionable. Either group is less likely to shop for quality or practical considerations.

The Need for Examination

Examination is indispensable in selecting old furniture. There is no substitute for it. Relying on an item's attractive outward appearance, its price, or a dealer's reputation is a mistake. The kind of inspection most buyers engage in, due to lack of information and perhaps too much schooling in the social graces, is a token effort much like kicking the tires of a used car. What is needed in its place is a thorough process that assesses practical needs, especially the need for repair and refinishing. Being thorough in an examination is the closest to a guarantee most buyers ever get.

Unless you enjoy doing extensive repair and refinishing work, it is important to buy furniture in good or easily restorable condition. There will almost always be more to do than is initially recognized. You may find something of value in shabby condition and decide the results outweigh the hard work, only to have to set the piece aside for long hours when your patience is worn out. At least a fourth of the furniture that is now available belongs in this category.

The Varieties of Authenticity

Another thing to consider in examining old furniture is *authenticity*. One kind of authenticity is the already mentioned use of materials that are what they seem. A second kind is the general idea of faithfulness to detail in decoration or construction methods. Any piece that is too watered down in these respects, unless its overall symmetry is improved, is too cheaply functional. A third authenticity concerns repair and refinishing. Although you probably won't be as fussy as a museum or a connoisseur, you are likely to want any repair and refinishing work to be much in keeping with the original character of any furniture you buy.

Survey First

Shopping for and comparing as wide a range of old furniture as possible is helpful in several respects. Even assuming that there is such a thing as beginner's luck, some preliminary survey work is more likely to produce success in finding desirable items.

Shopping is definitely a good way to compare styles, construction quality, repair and refinishing differences, and types of wood. Of course you can overdo things and engage in more surveying than is necessary. You'll have to decide at what point an investigation begins to kill your fun, but this is not likely to be as much a problem as having too little background experience.

Generalities

One thing you may encounter very early in shopping is that many things are being sold as simply old. It is a tireless tactic that assumes you are very naive. Similar ploys are to be found on other scores. Be cautious with all sorts of generalizations and clichés. They are very pervasive and sure to confront you when you begin to discuss old furniture. Some of the more glib ones include:

"You pay for what you get"
"The best woods are walnut and
      mahogany"
"You can't make a silk purse from a sow's
      ear"
"Don't buy painted furniture"

Generalizations are tricky. For every one that clearly will not hold water, there are several more that have enough truth in them to catch people off guard. Some generalizations, of course, sound neat when they fit a given situation, but many times they only appear to fit and are forced into use by something that is compelling about them, especially a catchy phrase. Appropriately or not, generalizations guide many buying decisions. Finding the exceptions to them, on the other hand, can be one of the pleasures of shopping.

Places to Buy

In general there are two places to buy old furniture: antique shops and auctions. Although the greatest source has traditionally been shop dealers, auctions are becoming a larger vehicle. In a time of rising prices, either setting is likely to require some buying sophistication. In any buying circumstance one of the things that will always be helpful is a knowledge of market prices. Another, of course, is knowing what you can afford.

Dealers and auctions are unusual because they take you away from retail selling and buying. At antique shops and flea markets there is usually a possibility of bargaining for prices. Auctions, on the other hand, offer the temptation of low prices in a climate with a quick tempo and a measure of distraction.

Restoring Things Yourself

Although many old furniture pieces are already refinished, others require some measure of work, and the amount varies greatly. If you like doing repair and refinishing, there is a great potential for satisfaction and an opportunity for reducing overall costs.

The one thing that is necessary to begin furniture work is a combination of patience, care, and perseverance. Most other matters, including tool knowledge, can be learned from books. Three things that will definitely help in a restoration project are a good refinishing and repair book for reference, outlining each small step of your project in sequence, and using sample tests in refinishing (to test stain, varnish, etc.).

The scope of furniture work is usually not very great in your first one or two items. Success with them makes any further articles easier. Some of the best refinishing is done as a social occasion. With a few laughs even stripping can be pleasant.

Using Old Furniture

A main concern of the book is buying furniture with use in mind. Considerable discussion will deal with fit, comfort, and other things related to physical use. A large part of chapter 6, the repair chapter, will deal with physical use almost systematically. A few remarks in other chapters will deal with room size, color, and coordinating old things with more modern furniture.

Styles

Even though the main focus of the book will be on shopping, examination, repairs, and refinishing, the next two chapters will center on styles. In the first chapter the various kinds of Victorian furniture will be considered, while in the next, the styles made between 1900 and 1945 will be discussed.

Styles are the most obvious things that differentiate old furniture. Knowing the various types that were produced gives you an idea of the range of quality and keeps you from venerating just any old piece. It also makes styles mundane enough to prevent your being too glued to the aesthetic side of furniture.

2

Furniture Styles: 1830–1900

This and the following chapter will deal with furniture styles between 1830 and 1945—from about the beginning of the machine age to the end of World War II. Not every style will be considered, just the ones that are generally affordable. For the most part this means that period (art) furniture, about which there is already so much written, will be discussed less, while factory furniture, of which there was enormously more made, will be treated accordingly. Country furniture, another type produced in great quantities, will also be discussed. After a background of the Victorian age and some basics about furniture styles in general, this particular chapter will focus on the individual styles from 1830 to 1900.

The Victorian Age

This chapter is essentially a look at the furniture of the Victorian era. The dates in the chapter title are a rounding off of Victoria's actual reign (1837 to 1901). Although she and her husband, Prince Albert, were great supporters of technological growth, the Victorian label had little to do with any influence exerted by the queen on furniture itself. It is based more on the fact that the beginning and end of her reign happened to coincide approximately with significant events in the history of furniture design and construction.

The Victorian era was a period of reviving *old* furniture styles. It ended only when new ones began to be created around 1900.

The revived styles reflected a variety of historical influences, most of them from the previous centuries of English and French furniture. Although old styles were revived, very few were redone in their original forms. The new versions were the result of new design processes, nearly all of them a consequence of the coming of the machine about 1830. This is an arbitrary but widely used date for the beginning of the Victorian era.

The Machine and Other Changes

One of the major changes brought by the machine was a new role for design. While formerly design was based on tradition and the experience and artistic sensibilities of the hand craftsman, during the Victorian age it became more and more subject to the capacities of the machine. The impact of the machine was gradual, however. Although it began as early as 1810 with the invention of the circular saw, it was only barely felt by 1830 and was not widespread until several decades later.

A major influence that combined with the machine was specialized labor. Specialized labor by itself was nothing new. It had begun in England and France in the 1700s with factories employing three and four hundred workers. Although it had begun early, it needed the machine and other industrial forces to develop in order to become widespread. Another important ingredient, the assembly line, also developed during Victorian times, although it had begun earlier.

Most, but not all Victorian furniture was made in factories using power tools. Hand tools continued to be used for country furniture and most art pieces. Although machines were available, their operation required a power source, either running water or steam. Few individuals, even if they could buy the equipment, could afford the additional expense. Some basic machine processes, especially rough sawing and planing, were utilized, however, when individual craftsmen could buy partially processed lumber from saw mills having the necessary power.

Combined Technologies

Before a virtual machine dominance was reached, methods that involved both hand and machine processes were used in furniture production, even in the factories. Many types of furniture parts were shaped roughly by machine and finished by hand; many tools were in use that were operated by foot or hand power. Some of the furniture that used a combined technology were the gothic, Elizabethan, cottage, and French revival styles. Later styles became more and more the product of machine operations alone.

A Changing Agriculture

A significant factor in an evolving industrial expansion was an increased mechanization in agriculture. Increased agricultural output brought about by new farm implements meant fewer jobs in a vocation with only a fixed demand for its products. On the other hand, many factory products were becoming in demand above necessity levels.

An increased demand for factory goods called for increased production and more labor. People living on farms who had neither the land nor the equipment to increase their own production soon moved to the industrial centers, usually the large cities. In the cities they were joined by millions of immigrants arriving from Europe. Although wages were very low, factory work for many of the new wage earners meant an unaccustomed security. It also provided the means for buying some of the new commodities for themselves.

The Buying Public

One of the reasons for the success of the industrial revolution and the furniture it produced was the feeling of awe it created in the buying public. The new technology was capable of manufacturing huge quantities of goods that were generally very well made and available at prices far cheaper than for hand-constructed articles. The new styles and construction features produced by the machines were also impressive.

Whenever the public's desire for the new goods began to diminish, advertising was created to revive it. Although in its day it was sometimes considered too forward, most of the advertising of the nineteenth century was more rational and used less psychology than today's methods. It was not entirely sincere but it did attempt to inform the buyer about the goods represented. Sometimes it was very long-winded as in this 1897 Sears catalog caption.

Treadle-operated jigsaw; a tool used in the transition from manual to engine power.

This table when closed has a 42 x 42-inch top and is made of the very finest selected and kiln-dried ash, both top, rims and legs. The rim of this table . . . is plain. We have persuaded the manufacturer, however, to make a special feature of this table for our customers, in the way of decoration, and the purchaser will find it very much more handsome than the one shown in the illustration, from the fact that the one which we shall ship will have fancy ornamentation and moulding on the rim. The legs are of extra strength and are fancy turned and carved, while the center panel and cross pieces are also decorated and carved. This table, as shown in the illustration has six legs, with a complete set of fine patent castors. We pack all our tables carefully, so that there will be no danger of rubbing or scratching, and the customer may be sure of receiving the goods in the best of condition. The finish is beautiful, being our best gloss finish, equal to the polish finish of other factories. . . .

1897 Sears Roebuck Catalog.
New York: Chelsea House, 1968, p. 643.

Role of the Railroad

The tremendous growth of the railroad in the 1800s was a fundamental force in creating an expanded market. In many instances it cut transportation to a tenth of the time it took horse-drawn wagons, and enabled several of the foundations of a complex industrial market to develop. Because of shorter transportation times and the increased amounts of freight that could be shipped in railroad boxcars, industrial companies began to set up systems of distributorship and wholesaling that made shipment to the consumer much easier, faster, and cheaper.

Once bulk transportation became available, retail merchandising began to develop in areas that had previously been too remote from the factories. The establishment of general stores and specialty shops that were closer to home provided a variety of ready-to-be-seen-and-purchased goods. In rural areas catalog sales grew because of the railroad's improvement of the postal service and delivery times in general.

A Belief in Progress

The Victorian age, because of its changes, was one of firm belief in progress. Great developments in scientific knowledge were one source of inspiration but were not universally felt or accepted. The main contributors to the belief in progress were the new and better goods derived from innovative technology and dynamic increases in production. Because of them, a tangibly better life appeared in everyone's dreams and expectations. Most Victorians were proud of the industrial accomplishments and felt a continued growth was destined.

New Social Classes

In addition to the optimism it created, the industrial revolution was also responsible for the economic rise of the middle class. Through the new jobs it created, it provided enough in wages to lift millions of people out of near poverty. An improved income not only increased buying power, but also, in turn, perpetuated the growth of the factories because of the increased demand for goods. Several aspects of industrial growth had a dynamic effect. One of the great consequences was a change in the pace of life. The speed of obtainable ambitions and the speed of meeting production quotas led to new life styles, both exciting and harried.

A new upper class also developed out of the improved economy and its opportunities. Merchants, bankers, and other businessmen became wealthy almost overnight. As the newly rich sought the refinements of the established upper class, possessions became the great value. With an increased wealth, status and accumulation replaced simple good taste. It was said that when the efforts of the newly rich only captured the obvious, fancier characteristics of what they sought, vulgarity had become popular.

Elaboration

The Victorian period was one of elaboration rather than simplicity. If Jean Paul Sartre was right when he wrote that one of the basic motives of human personality is to fill all types of voids, the Victorians were the champions of the desire. Much of the Victorian decoration, in contrast with earlier times, was made separately from the main body of an item of furniture and then glued and tacked in place. Everything from kitchen utensils to furniture to heavy industrial equipment was decorated in some way, if only with pinstripes; many things were decorated to the hilt. If an item was bare it was considered cheap and inartistic.

Out-Distancing Taste

To a large degree the increased ornament of the Victorians was a result of a rapid economic and technological growth out-distancing taste. People with improved new wages or overnight wealth were quick to grab for the obvious, more gaudy forms of decoration. The new demand brought about a vast production of goods ornamented in a mixture of styles. To the manufacturers, one benefit of glued-on ornaments was the ease of shuffling designs by combining different furniture bodies. New styles could be produced with little retooling or other steps in production.

The Victorian House

The typically decorated Victorian house was as gaudy as its furniture styles. Frequently it was oversized, with large rooms having high ceilings; the walls were often papered with overstated floral patterns or murals. When paint was used, some of the popular colors were lilac, mauve, purple, blue, brown, and forest green. Often the paint was little more than a colored whitewash and quickly became dim. Another kind of painting administered to mantels, banisters, and other woodwork was fake graining, usually applied over pine or poplar to resemble rosewood or golden oak.

The draperies in Victorian homes were typically heavy, opaque, and had sewed-on tassels or fringe. Small valances called *lambrequins* were draped on bookcases, mantels, and just about anything else with an edge to be decorated. Tables and chairs were often skirted with pleated material having a wide bottom fringe.

In the way of upholstery, the favorite fabrics for the opulent look were velvets, velours, brocades, satins, and a deeper pile variety called *plush*. The lower-status fabric was *horsehair*, a hard, smooth material especially used on inexpensive parlor furniture. The gaudiest furniture, of which little survives because of its fragile nature, was of papier mâché highly decorated with painted designs.

The center of Victorian social life was the parlor. Even small houses had one, while large houses had both a front parlor for more formal occasions and a back parlor for everyday relaxation and meeting with close friends. The front parlor was the showcase and the means of impressing the boss, the preacher, and the priggish old lady from down the street.

More Elaboration

Victorians routinely accumulated large numbers of decorative items. They called such items *bibelots* and their variety and number have never been approached in any other era. Here is a list of some that were fairly commonplace:

cast-metal cranes and herons
Chinese embroideries
decorative vases
dried flowers
dried grass
family albums
family Bibles
framed mottos and scriptural quotations
Japanese fans
medieval weapons and armor

moose heads
porcupine quills
sea shells
statuettes
waxed flowers

Another name for the collected objects was bric-a-brac, and it was displayed on mantels, bookcases, whatnots, and pianos. The motivation for bric-a-brac was strong because several factors were behind it. First there was Sartre's elaboration drive, present in most cultures, but in the Victorian era all of a sudden given a wealth of new and inexpensive machine-produced goods. Much of the elaboration drive was an emphasis on quantity supported by few guidelines for the selection and artistic arrangement of things. A clutter also resulted from the confusion brought by rapid social and style changes. The pleasure of possessing things was more easily acquired than a sense of proportion.

Victorian machine-made furniture, like its bibelots, was enormously popular. One reason for its sales volume was the furniture establishment's part in creating an ever-changing fashion. New styles were presented almost yearly to outmode the old ones and increase sales. For the first time in a big way the new had become the good. For some critics the yearly parade of fashion was disturbing, however. They felt that some sort of stability was needed.

The Moral Alternative

The critics of Victorian furniture had emerged as early as mid century when some of the machine and fashion trends were becoming obvious. Most of the critics were Englishmen looking at similar trends in their own country. Almost all of them began calling for an honest use of materials, a limit to ornamentation, and a return to hand methods. With John Ruskin, William Morris, and several others, furniture design and construction suddenly became matters of morality.

Many people were ready for moral lessons. After Charles Eastlake, an Englishman, published *Hints on Household Taste* in 1872, he became very widely read in America. Eastlake, while critical of machine methods, offered no new style as an alternative. He advocated, rather, a return to an earlier English style, the *Jacobean*, a design he considered the best example of honest construction and simple decoration. Eastlake was too late, however. While his ideas were of interest to many, they basically called for a return to hand-constructed furniture, most of which would have been much more expensive than the available factory products. Ironically, Eastlake's own particular style preferences became diluted in cheapened commercial versions of pieces illustrated in his book. No new style was to develop until about 1900.

Style Matters

Most of this chapter and the next one will deal with individual furniture styles. Although there will be enough background presented with each of them to give a broad perspective, some knowledge of styles in general is needed as a starting point.

Style Themes

Almost all furniture styles can be fitted into broad categories of design according to their proportions and shapes and according to what kind of decoration, if any, was used. The broad themes below are the

Classical simplicity and balance expressed in a piece sometimes referred to in the nineteenth century as a plain dresser.

main ones practiced throughout history and cover the great majority of all American furniture, even including modern items.

Classicism — Classicism relates to styles that are based on the architectural forms and symbols of ancient Greece and Rome. The term applies to several specific styles in the late eighteenth and early nineteenth centuries, especially the works of Adams and Hepplewhite. It also applies to some of the revival styles of the Victorian era and even to some of the shapes in modern furniture. A more general meaning of classicism relates to furniture design that has proportions that are traditional, fairly simple, and balanced in symmetry. Compared with the extremes of the baroque and ro-

coco styles, classicism is very controlled. It attempts to follow the ideal rather than seek free expression.

Baroque — The main characteristic in the baroque theme is exaggeration. The decoration is always overdone and frequently out of scale with the overall size of the furniture. Usually there are large curves involved. Baroque is considered a masculine theme because its decorations are large. The most recent examples of it are in some of the Victorian styles and massive combination furniture made from about 1925 to 1945.

Rococo — Rococo is considered a feminine theme because its decorations are more delicate. Its fullest expression was in

Baroque themes expressed in the large curves and ornament of a renaissance bed.

some of the eighteenth- and nineteenth-century French styles named for several of the Louis kings. With those styles there was an emphasis on accurately carved plant and animal forms *(naturalism)*, and on rich, asymmetrical curves. Recent styles having just the rococo curves are bentwood chairs, some pieces of wicker, and some of the simpler pieces of massive combination furniture of the twenties and thirties. The term *rococo* is sometimes interchanged with *baroque* because both are ornate and have curves.

Functionalism — In the pure meaning of

this term, furniture designs are based on utilitarian purposes rather than aesthetics. Practicality and comfort are dominant considerations and there is little if any decoration. Primitive country furniture was made almost entirely along these lines. Modern furniture, although it strives hard to be functional, has evolved into a highly developed art emphasizing beauty of form and materials. Shape and materials are as important as practicality.

Style Elements

There are broad themes in furniture styles and then there are individual styles. The characteristics that combine to form an individual style are called *motifs*. Most of them fall into one of the following categories: materials used, finish applied, overall form, construction features, or decoration.

Although each of the first four elements is important with one style or another, the last one, decoration, is the main way that furniture styles, particularly the Victorian, differ. Some decorative motifs that are probably familiar are pointed gothic arches, Chippendale ball and claw feet, and the pressed gingerbread carvings of the golden oak era. Other decorative motifs may take the form of carvings, inlay work, turnings, applied ornaments, etc. Hundreds of specific motifs have been used in furniture.

Some styles have many motifs, others just a few. Whatever the number, most individual pieces have only some of those that collectively belong to their styles. Factory pieces, of which there are several examples in the following pages, generally have motifs that are watered down and sparse in number.

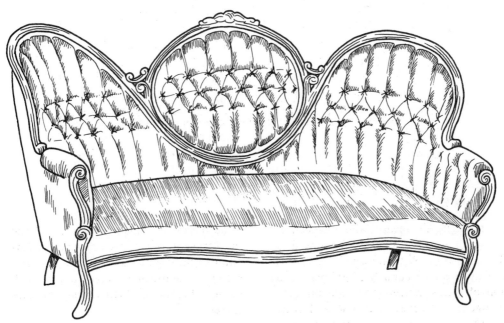

Rococo sofa emphasizing asymmetrical curves.

Style Time Frames

The dates to be discussed with each of the styles in this and the next chapter are for the periods of time during which each was especially popular. This is not to say that each one was isolated in a neat time frame as is often implied, for instance, in a discussion of period furniture. Very few styles came and went abruptly. Many, in fact, continued to be producd for years beyond the time in which they flourished. Some styles, even though they died out for a while, were later revived in the form of reproductions.

Another matter of significance is that particular styles did not exist alone during their period of popularity. They were overlapped by others. It was not unusual, especially during the Victorian era, for four or more styles all to be popular at the same time. As is the case now, a variety existed to satisfy a population with different tastes and pocketbooks.

Style Modifiers

Most of the furniture that will be discussed in this chapter is not pure in style. The Victorian era began a departure from pure styles as no other period before it. Several practices in design modification accounted for it.

Eclecticism, the combining of elements from different styles, was frequently practiced by hand craftsmen and became widespread with factory items. In such cases, and to take advantage of recognized historic forms of decoration, motifs having a hint or more of familiarity to the buying public were assembled from separate styles. In its most commercial form eclecticism involved a nearly indiscriminate use of glued-on ornaments and other furniture parts used mainly for cost expedience.

Stylizing, a process often used to create a semblance of authenticity, was the watering down of traditional motifs. (The word *simplified* means about the same as stylized.) Through reducing an original to a less detailed form, costs could be lowered. Frequently the process was so overdone that it is more accurate to say that the derived furniture was simply inspired by the original models rather than stylized. Sometimes, on the positive side, more appealing motifs with simpler lines were created.

Eclecticism and stylizing were the main trends away from pure styles. Another process, *interpretation*, involved style changes to add a new touch to old motifs. Often there was a production advantage in the process. *Elaboration*, a practice similar to interpretation, meant the expansion of motifs, giving them greater extension in size, number, or diversity. While many of the changes were slight and conservative, others were wholesale and almost indiscriminate.

Country Furniture

The phrase *country furniture* covers a lot. Although much of it was made by rural furniture makers and carpenters, the label usually includes almost *any* handmade furniture that was constructed for ordinary use rather than for art's sake. Up until the great surge of furniture factories in the late 1800s, most furniture was in a country category. Much of it began as plainer designs of English period styles, the simplification needed to make it achievable by most craftsmen and affordable to their customers. Others came directly from or evolved out of the country furniture brought by

An eclectic sideboard without unity of design in its decorations. It deserves to be called "hodgepodge eclectic."

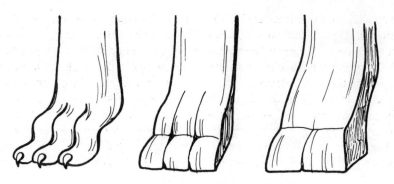

Steps in a continued stylizing of the lion's paw.

immigrant craftsmen from Germany, France, and Holland. Some pieces with immigrant influences went on to become American classics, which usually are regarded as entirely native.

A special class of country furniture, *primitives*, consists of pieces that are characteristically crudely made and are almost purely functional. Although primitives are abundant, it is inaccurate to think of them as the main body of country furniture. Many country items have attractive designs and required as much skill as many period pieces. An amazing look at the complexity of the craft of making country furniture is Aldren Watson's *Country Furniture* (New York: New American Library, 1974).

During the mid-1800s there was a great overlap of country designs and *cottage furniture* (one of the earliest styles made in factories). Some country furniture was taken up by factories and some cottage designs were copied by country craftsmen.

The wood species most associated with country furniture are pine and poplar, but almost every other was used as well. The choice of species in a particular geographic area depended on its own timber supply and its taste.

With cheaper woods, especially the softer ones, country furniture was usually painted. Often the paint was made from milk combined with natural vegetable or mineral dyes. (This was the milk paint that has become so popularized.) The most frequent paint color was probably *poor man's mahogany*, a very dark red. Over better woods the choice of finish was usually either shellac or linseed oil.

Country furniture was made for every room in the house. A higher proportion of country kitchen pieces to be found today is due to the fact that city kitchens also had the same functional-looking furniture. A lower proportion of parlor-type country pieces is due to the lack of parlors in many, if not most country houses.

A great amount of country furniture is still available, particularly through auctions. Needless to say it varies a lot in condition and quality. Kitchen and other utilitarian pieces have generally seen lots of use and need extra examination. One of country furniture's largest advantages, because of its plainer lines and lack of carving or other decoration, is its compatibility with many other furniture styles.

Despite a relatively humble overall status, some country furniture is expensive. Pie safes, corner cupboards, and large hutches often cost much more than their functional value. Very often country furniture was not poor in construction or materials. Pieces made of walnut generally bring high prices and are in great demand. For an in-depth shopper's look at country furniture, see Thomas Voss's *Antique American Country Furniture* (Philadelphia: Lippincott, 1978).

Shaker Furniture
(1779–1900)

After a short period of beginnings in England, the religious group that was to be known as the Shakers arrived in America in 1774. The leader of the group, Mother Ann Lee, who was considered the personage of Christ in his second coming, guided the establishment of the first Shaker community near Albany, New York, in 1779.

The Shaker religion, from its earliest development, was one of self-denial, self-sufficiency, and withdrawal from the outside world. It viewed work as worship and the means to an achievable paradise on earth. Neatness in every endeavor, was viewed as next to godliness. The furniture developed by the religious group was made to reflect its values and was intended to be essentially functional. One of the guiding statements of Shaker philosophy was, "That which has in itself the highest use possesses the greatest beauty." The Shaker furniture style was partly a rejection of the ornateness in the styles of ordinary society. Any form of decoration was considered frivolous because it went beyond a strictly utilitarian form.

There was room for beauty in Shaker furniture, but it was beauty of form rather than decoration. The formal artistry of

the Shakers developed out of their desire to make things "perfect unto their purpose." They believed in excelling the outside world in "works that are truly virtuous and useful to man in this life. . . ."

Aside from making furniture for their own use, the Shakers, as early as 1789, began selling some goods to local merchants. Chairs were one of their specialties. In all cases the designs were sturdy

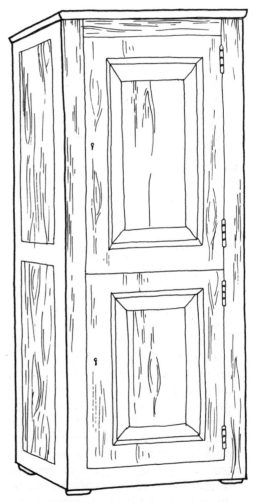

A heavy country cupboard with two compartments (probably used for kitchen storage).

A popular country cabinet, sometimes known as a jelly cupboard.

where necessary, but slim and trim where strength was not important; there is a definite slightness to Shaker furniture compared with other styles. The Shakers' reasoning was that since they expected to take special care with it, any extra bulk was unnecessary.

There is a great similarity between Shaker and much country furniture, the main difference being the lesser bulk of the Shaker designs. Undoubtedly there were instances where one directly affected the design of the other. Shaker pieces, rather than being completely original, were often refinements of prevailing country forms. Another rea-

son for their similarity was that both were designed for utility.

Genuine Shaker-made furniture is expensive and seldom found. Reproductions are available, however, for those who want the design and aren't concerned with age. Occasionally pieces of country furniture with very similar designs are available.

Pillar and Scroll Furniture (1830–1855)

Pillar and scroll furniture is usually referred to as *Late Empire*. It is a highly stylized version of the American Empire art

A primitive country table with parts shaped roughly by hand.

Pillar and scroll was one of the most prolific styles of the nineteenth century. It first gained popularity in the 1830s through its sales by Joseph Meeks and Sons, a New York manufacturer. It was adopted as a particularly easy production style after the publication of John Hall's *Cabinet Maker's Assistant* in 1840. In the book Hall showed factory owners the ease of making scrolls and a wealth of specific designs to

furniture that preceded it in this country. The very first Empire style had begun in France as almost the official furniture of Napoleon's reign. Napoleon, in his conceit, associated himself with the great ancient civilizations of Greece, Rome, and Egypt and preferred motifs taken from their artifacts. Such things as torches, laurel wreaths, and sphinxes were part of the French Empire design. American Empire, which followed the French, kept some of the motifs and added others germane to American patriotism. The bald eagle in its different displays was perhaps the most frequent.

Our main subject here, Late Empire, in contrast with the earlier forms, is so simplified that it has almost no motifs. Almost the only ones are S and C scrolls and pillars highly diluted from ancient architectural decorations. Late Empire is so consistently and thoroughly based on these motifs that it is entirely appropriate to call it pillar and scroll furniture. Most of it to be found is veneered.

A country corner cupboard expressing refinement in design and details.

An elegant Shaker rocker. Function of the top rung was for hanging the rocker on pegs during large group gatherings and for floor cleaning.

Missing veneer is important to look for in examining pieces of this style. Although replacing veneer with an appropriate thickness is a significant problem, a greater one is getting it to match well in grain and color. Another problem is one of gluing and clamping broken scrolls; it is often difficult to clamp anything curved. One other thing to consider is the size of pillar and scroll pieces. Many were made in massive proportions suited only for large Victorian houses.

Windsor Chairs and Boston Rockers (Dates Not Sufficiently Clear)

Windsor chairs originated in England in the early 1700s and quickly became favorites in the colonies. In America, although an essential ingredient of a curved back

copy. The style caught on everywhere and remained popular up into the 1850s. Toward the end of the century it was revived and continued in production through the 1920s.

Whether machines were involved in the early production of this style has been a matter of debate. While some writers consider pillar and scroll furniture the first thoroughgoing machine style, others argue that the band saw, the power tool credited with the rise of the style, was not invented until 1865 or so and could not have produced the furniture made earlier. The issue is, of course, mainly academic. Most pillar and scroll furniture now available, in fact, was made after the turn of the century.

Small Shaker table emulating beauty of form more than most other designs.

A scroll hall table. Why the mirror is down so low is a mystery.

Pillar and scroll table with veneer on most outer surfaces. Sometimes the veneer was rosewood. Usually, though, it was various cuts of mahogany.

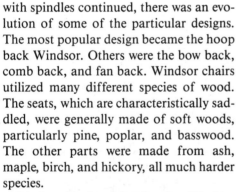

with spindles continued, there was an evolution of some of the particular designs. The most popular design became the hoop back Windsor. Others were the bow back, comb back, and fan back. Windsor chairs utilized many different species of wood. The seats, which are characteristically saddled, were generally made of soft woods, particularly pine, poplar, and basswood. The other parts were made from ash, maple, birch, and hickory, all much harder species.

Produced by hand for decades, Windsor chairs became factory commodities in the mid 1800s and have continued to be made up through the present as reproductions. During the early 1900s Windsors that were very stylized became popular for kitchen use. Usually they had fewer spindles and less saddle in the seats. Most of them were

A hoop back Windsor with saddled seat. Millions of these were made as reproductions after 1900.

originally painted and have accumulated additional coats over the years.

There are two chair designs that have partially evolved from the Windsor. One is the *captain's chair* with its dramatically curved back. Captain's chairs for a variety of uses were popular from the middle of the 1800s and were usually made of oak.

The other borrowed design is the *Boston rocker*. The arms, legs, spindles, and rungs of the Boston rocker are Windsor in design. The seat and the top of the back both have scroll shapes taken from *fancy chairs*, a style popular in the early part of the 1800s. Like fancy chairs, Boston rockers are sten-

A Boston rocker.

cil-decorated with fruit and flower motifs on the seat and back.

Elizabethan Revival (1830–1840)

To the Victorians, any furniture that was English and really old was called *Jacobean* or *Elizabethan*. One particular style given the Elizabethan name actually had motifs from furniture made under Charles II (1660–1685). It borrowed only a few motifs and only pieces from a few rooms were involved. The dominant motif in Elizabethan revival pieces is a ball and spiral turning used in legs and other parts. The main items to be found are dining room

An early captain's chair of a style found frequently in New England.

buffets, tables, and chairs; library tables were made in significant numbers also. The chairs typically have no arms and their backs are either carved or covered with needlepoint tapestry. Their profile consists of a very low seat and a very high back.

The Elizabethan revival is considered to have had an effect on another style, *cottage spool furniture* (see "Cottage Furniture" below). There was a second revival of the more properly Elizabethan when it was made from oak near the end of the century. The spiral motif became present in

Thonet's number 14 chair with a cane bottom. Embossed wooden bottoms were used in other versions.

cabinets, library tables, and several other kinds of furniture.

Bentwood Furniture
(1830 through Present)

The first efficient method for bending wood was introduced by Michael Thonet in Austria in 1830. Thonet had developed a special process using steam and quick-release metal clamps. His choice of wood,

An Elizabethan-style chair having the major motifs.

which he usually finished with dark stain or paint, was *beech*. Thonet was joined by his five sons in 1853. (The firm is still in business.) It began and has continued producing a large number of furniture designs, chiefly chairs. One chair that was especially popular, no. 14, is said to have sold fifty million copies by 1910.

The Thonet style, imitated by many different companies both then and now, is considered rococo because of the curves found in most designs. In America, bentwood chairs, although departing little from the Thonet shapes (except in the Windsor varieties), were usually made from birch and oak instead of beech.

Cottage Furniture
(1840–1880)

In Victorian times there were two meanings of the term *cottage furniture*. The general meaning was any furniture that was more suited to small country houses than to the large, many-roomed residences of the Victorian upper classes. In a snobbish sense cottage furniture meant anything that was cheap and highly stylized. Included were factory-made country pieces that were fake-grained and country furniture in general.

The more specific meaning of cottage furniture was a label applied to either of two distinct styles made by some of the earliest furniture factories. One style, always referred to as just plain cottage furniture, was usually made from pine or poplar and was painted either white, gray, yellow, lilac, or light blue. Painted decorations were often added in the form of flowers and fruits, and thin pinstriping was done to frame some of the rectangular surfaces. Another motif sometimes used was halved spindles applied to the fronts of chests and dressers. This particular cot-

tage style was almost entirely bedroom furniture. Some pieces had marble tops.

The other cottage style was called *spool-turned furniture*. It was the style considered to have been influenced by the turnings of the Elizabethan revival. Largely based on the capabilities of the lathe, spool-turned furniture mainly consisted of bedroom pieces and small parlor tables. A great amount of it was made, especially as reproductions that were manufactured during the first decades after 1900. Some of the spool motifs included stylized shapes

A cottage dresser with an especially ornate mirror. Compare with the renaissance dresser coming up later in this chapter.

similar to bobbins, knobs, spools, and sausages.

Spool-turned furniture was sometimes quality-constructed. Although usually made of poplar, often the wood was walnut, cherry, or maple. The poplar was usually stained. Probably the most popular single item of the spool-turned style was the Jenny Lind bed named after the Swedish soprano who toured the United States with P. T. Barnum during the mid 1800s.

Something important to consider is the type of stock used in spool-turned construction. The better spool-turned items have parts that are from single pieces of wood. Cheaper items, especially reproductions, are often made from several pieces glued together. Some of them tend to swell

A table of the spool variety having "sausage" motif legs.

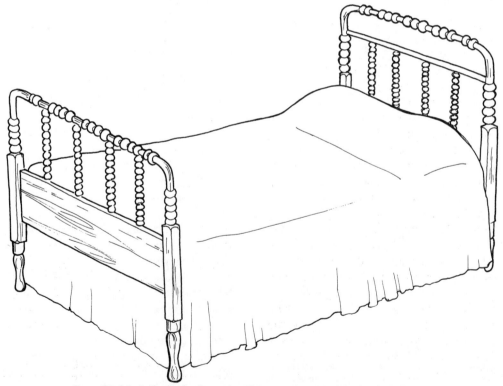

Jenny Lind bed. Probably the most widely reproduced bed in furniture history.

and come off, particularly in a dip-stripping process. Spool-turned furniture should not be confused with home handicraft furniture having real spools glued together. Although real spools are sometimes attractive, their assembly is usually weak.

Rustic Furniture
(1840–1930)

This style is without a doubt the oldest form of wooden furniture. Although made by home methods for thousands of years, it suddenly became popular enough in the mid 1800s to require mass production. One reason for its popularity was the attention given it by Andrew Jackson Downing, a tastemaking architect of the times

"Old Hickory" chair popular for decades. Named after Andrew Jackson, of whom it was said, "He bends but never breaks." Structural parts made of hickory.

who described and illustrated it in his book, *Cottage Residences*. Many things that were rustic, including houses, were popular around the turn of the century.

Most rustic furniture was made from tree trunks, limbs, and branches with the bark left on. Careful selection, cutting, and nailing were needed. The major wood used in rustic furniture was hickory. Around the turn of the century hickory branches were sometimes bent by steam into shapes inspired by the art nouveau style. An excellent book on the rustic style is Sue Stephenson's *Rustic Furniture* (New York: Van Nostrand, 1979).

Eclectic Furniture
(1840–1900)

Eclectic furniture is any that is a mixture of two or more styles. It was made throughout the entire Victorian period and rode a high crest of popularity whenever fashion was defined through the presence of motifs the buying public could vaguely associate with recognizable styles. Eclecticism succeeded most when there was an absence of styles that were fresh (practically the whole Victorian era). Something seemingly new could be created by combining old motifs or creating simple new ones.

With factory furniture eclecticism largely resulted from the use of machines that made it easy to produce motifs that could be applied, rather than made part of, basic furniture components. Many eclectic pieces, taking advantage of the add-on technology, were highly ornamented. Through eclecticism the separate French revival styles of Louis 15th and 16th were often combined. Some pieces, instead of mixing individual styles, combined the

An eclectic Victorian parlor set.

broad design themes of classicism, rococo, and baroque.

One particular sort of furniture that was eclecticized was the Victorian parlor set. The parlor set, with its upright seating, reflected the Victorian social values of formality and correctness. Many of the sets were made from birch or maple, two woods that, incidentally, present frequent stripping problems. Parlor sets will be discussed again later.

Probably the most eclecticized furniture of the 1800s was golden oak. Most golden oak, in fact, was a mixture of different designs. In addition to eclecticizing, the processes of stylizing, interpretation, and elaboration were also involved. Hardware, even more than other added-on parts, became a thing easily varied to produce different style versions.

The departures from pure designs that resulted from the different processes were mostly done for novelty, hyperfashion, and a display by manufacturers of their ability to produce an endless variety. A considerable amount of "odd" chairs and other furniture that was produced around the turn of the century was the extreme of

eclecticism. Many looked thrown together in design.

Some eclectic pieces are a hodgepodge, but some are not. The simpler ones constructed of quality woods, white oak in particular, have tasteful decoration that complements, rather than dominates the basic appearance.

French Revival (1845–1870)

The French revival styles, although mainly art furniture, are included here because they are a large part of today's stereotype of Victorian fanciness. They originated in France about 1830 as a return to the eighteenth-century styles of Louis 15th and 16th and began a subsequent period in the United States about 1845. The Louis 15th style, the largest part of the revival, was the most ornate. It was a style of both rococo form and decoration with a particular emphasis on curves. Some of its typical construction features were serpentine drawer fronts, oval shaped tabletops, curved X table stretchers, balloon back chairs, and cabriole legs.

Rococo decorations, as mentioned earlier, are mainly naturalistic. In the Louis 15th style there was usually a detailing of flowers, fruit, leaves, and tendrils. Other styles had animal designs as well. Rococo motifs are found in Louis 15th carving, applied decorations, and hardware.

The Louis 16th style returned to classical motifs. It replaced the rococo curves with straight lines and the naturalistic decorations with simple ones from architecture. Another feature was *incised lines* (much like the decorations in cut glass). A motif used in both the Louis 15th and

16th styles was *finger molding*, grooves approximately ¼ to ½ inch wide cut into the wood.

The French revival had its stylized and eclectic factory versions. In some pieces the different Louis styles were combined and sometimes had motifs from other styles mixed in also. The French revival, especially in its factory editions, brought the parlor set into its greatest popularity. The parlor set was a grouping of matched pieces and usually consisted of three to eleven items with upholstered seats and backs. The individual pieces that could be purchased

A Louis 15th X stretcher table. This is a simple one with relatively little decoration.

A Louis 15th chair of fairly ornate design.

they were made of maple, birch, or mixed woods.

Be careful of buying lady's chairs of whatever style. Some are much too small for today's use. Some of them, also, are uncomfortably straight. Something else important about parlor sets is that, even if their springs and webbing are in good condition (which they very frequently are not), they can be quite expensive to have reupholstered. It is easy to invest five or more times the purchase price in refinishing and reupholstering many parlor sets.

Patent Furniture (1850–1900)

The last half of the nineteenth century was a great period of invention. Thou-

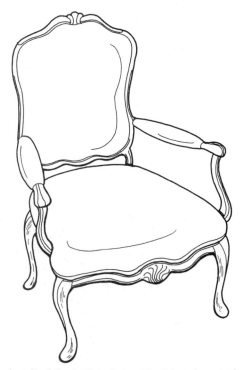

A stylized Louis 15th chair with all but the curved rococo shape gone.

were sofas, love seats, gentlemen's chairs (large and with arms), the lady's chairs (smaller and without arms in order to accommodate hooped skirts). Some sets also had dining and rocking chairs.

The furniture done in the French revival styles was not poorly made. In the early years of the revival, the more pure and expensive pieces were made of rosewood, mahogany, or walnut. Walnut was also used in the stylized furniture and was the wood usually found in parlor sets. French revival pieces were revived again after 1900. Often sands of patents were granted to all kinds of new devices, quite a few of them furniture. Most of the furniture patents were given for things with convertible features, provisions for self-storage, or mechanisms for adjustment. Beds were designed that were convertible into bookcases, tables, and even pianos. There were also many versions of the reclining chair, sometimes complete with a pull-out foot rest. All kinds of swivel chairs and platform rockers were invented. The director's chair, available in a collapsible form very much like today's, was patented in 1852. A few kinds of tables with self-storing leaves were made.

There is not a great deal of patent furniture that survives. Much of it was made with insufficient sturdiness and was constructed mainly for experimentation or novelty. The requirements for obtaining a patent were not as strict in those days. Patent furniture that is found should be examined for true usefulness and to see if all the parts are on hand.

A renaissance cabinet executed by Leon Marcotte. Less detail is shown than in the original. Very ornate.

A patented lounging chair with rudimentary footrest; Lazy Boy's distant ancestor.

Victorian Renaissance (1860–1880)

This is another of the styles that at least in its art furniture, has contributed to a stereotype of Victorian ornateness. Rather than a new design, the style was a revival of the classical themes of the renaissance. Its revival was inspired by nineteenth-century excavations of ancient ruins in Greece and Italy. Because little actual furniture was found, most of the motifs used were borrowed from the remains of architecture. Some of the motifs were:

acanthus—leaf moldings
pilasters—half-round or rectangular columns
rinceau—continuous spiral or wavy ornament, sometimes intertwined with stems and leaves

The most important designer of renaissance art pieces was Leon Marcotte, an immigrant cabinetmaker who is credited with the cabinet in the illustration. Marcotte's work incorporated many of the renaissance motifs.

Although there were many motifs in the art furniture, the stylized factory pieces, which were produced in far greater numbers, usually had only a few. The illustration shows a typical dresser displaying some of the frequent kinds. If there is a common denominator in renaissance factory furniture, it is the presence of semi-

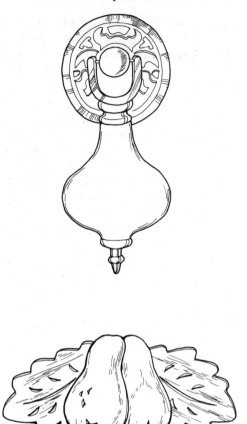

A renaissance dresser emphasizing much curvature. These were often massive in size and proportion. Expressive of baroque themes.

The two main styles of renaissance drawer pulls.

circular curvature in some aspect of an item's decoration. The curvature is often done in large, baroque proportions.

Factory pieces of this style are often so watered down that they are sometimes distinguished as "Grand Rapids Renaissance," the name taken from the city that was becoming the furniture capital of the Midwest during the time the style was popular. While Grand Rapids at first made furniture that was in the art category, it later became more and more diluted. Parlor sets in both detailed and stylized designs were common in the Grand Rapids style.

Most quality renaissance furniture is walnut, often with marble tops on dressers, chests, and tables. Other pieces, fewer in number, were made of ash, poplar, and pine. Fake graining was often used on the softer woods but has seldom survived in good condition. The hardware used on renaissance furniture is fairly consistent. Drawer pulls have either a teardrop design combining brass and black-painted wood or are made of walnut in a carved cluster of fruit.

Turkish and Moorish Furniture (1870–1880)

When the mystique of the Middle East was introduced to the world at the time of the building of the Suez Canal, many people had to have something reflecting its culture. Somehow the idea of setting off a section of the house got started. This became known as the *Turkish corner* or *Moorish den*. Almost thrown into one of them were many exotic trappings including embroideries, oriental rugs, and some amount of cushioned furniture with fringes, tufting, and tassels—all surrounded by folding screens or tent awnings of the desert. The reigning sheik of it all was the wealthy American businessman, tired from work and escaping to his stylish, cushioned comforts.

Although this fanciful decorating style borrowed from many countries, it is usually labeled Turkish or Moorish because

A Turkish den, sometimes known as a *cozy corner*.

of the dominance of the two particular cultures in the style. The Turkish contribution was its upholstered furniture. Its popularity, in fact, gave rise to many American factories and helped establish the upholstery business in this country.

With the Turkish style, upholstery took a new direction toward *overstuffed* furniture, the bulging kind that almost entirely shows fabric rather than wood. A very lavish stuffing and tufting was used in Turkish-inspired divans, couches, chairs, and ottomans. Ottomans made as circular sofas were one of the central pieces in this style. A contribution that was Moorish was the Damascus table, a delicately inlaid, six- or eight-sided creation about 18 inches wide. The Moorish influence had more to do with architecture than with furniture and was expressed more often in the walls and ceilings of wealthy homes.

It was the Turkish-Moorish corner, as much as anything else, that gave the Victorian era a reputation for clutter and overdoing things. The extravagances in it reflected the new wealth, a delight in new and unusual things, and a love of possessions.

Eastlake
(1870–1890)

When Charles Eastlake, the English architect, wrote *Hints on Household Taste* in 1868, he was especially against the ever-changing fashion facilitated by machine production and the ability of furniture merchants and manufacturers to make the buying public style-conscious through advertising. On one hand he saw an excess of luxury in the many curves and applied ornaments in the French and renaissance revivals; on the other he saw many cheap productions with poor joinery, inferior wood, and tacked-on parts.

An Eastlake chair showing spindles and the use of pegs to secure joints.

To Eastlake the furniture of the times lacked sincerity of expression and honesty in craftsmanship. Those, he felt, were matters of morality. His book, after it was published in America, became an immediate success. Eastlake's own furniture preferences, which were carried out more in England, were for a return to the aesthetic and construction principles in early Jacobean furniture (1603–1649). Named for James I of England, Jacobean was a blend of medieval and renaissance forms.

There are several earmarks for Eastlake's own choice of furniture. As it was faithfully produced in England, it emphasized square or rectangular shapes (the dominant motif), the use of pegged rather than screwed joints, a display of short spindles, and a further ornamentation through carvings, inlay, or decorated tiles.

It was a great irony when American furniture manufacturers got hold of the Eastlake style. By the time it occurred, Eastlake's movement had become so popularized and his concerns for sincerity and honesty so clichéd, that people clamored for anything with an Eastlake label.

Practically all of the Eastlake furniture made in America was done in factories. With broad interpretations from the English pieces, the square and rectangular shapes became emphasized with several types of linear grooves and other molding. Incised lines (those decorations done like cut glass) and rough chip carving were often thrown in without any regard for unity of

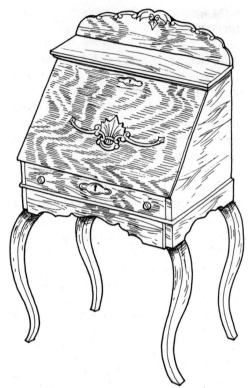

Small golden oak secretary or lady's desk. French motifs dominate.

An Eastlake dresser of American design. Much of the trim was painted black.

design. Some items having black or red geometric patterns and incised lines accentuated with gold paint are as gaudy as anything that is Victorian.

The woods to be found in American Eastlake are very good, mainly oak, walnut, cherry, and maple. Sometimes it is ebonized — either stained or painted black. It is ironic to see black stain over cherry or walnut, but it appears often in this furniture.

Some Eastlake bedroom pieces are very difficult to distingish from renaissance. Both have incised lines, linear grooves, and one or two other common features.

Golden Oak
(1875–1935)

Golden oak was not a single style but a great accumulation of motifs using oak or similar-looking woods in its manufacture. Decorative elements from many Victorian styles were borrowed. Usually the elements were highly simplified; interpretations and elaborations were rampant. In the evolution of golden oak styles many new types of them were created, most of them based on the special capabilities of the new power tools.

One power tool, the tracing carver, could duplicate many kinds of hand-cut designs and was especially instrumental in the production of new motifs. A motif frequently used in the backs of oak chairs was a facsimile of carving pressed into them by machine. The patterns produced were one type of decoration in a category that has become known as *gingerbread*. Others include simple chip carving, scroll-cut designs, and fancy trim moldings. Gingerbread, although it was not used in every case, was one of the chief ingredients of golden oak furniture.

The term *golden oak* started when the wood itself began to be finished either naturally or stained a golden yellow to simulate the wood's aged color. Formerly it had been finished in various dark shades according to the English tradition. The use of oak in American furniture, although it had been dormant for many decades, probably began with one of the English revival styles, perhaps the renaissance.

Oak had always been the most abundant hardwood in America. The reutilization of it that came with golden oak was a great windfall to the factories. According to Herbert Myrick, an enthusiastic writer commenting on the manufacture of oak in 1901 (which was about the peak of the golden oak style), the new technology was "creating a new industry that converted a hitherto waste product, unlimited in extent, into furniture, household furnishings, and other staple articles. . . ."

One of the reasons for golden oak's great popularity was that it was advertised as more democratic and affordable than the older, more ornate furniture. Because of its stylizing it was promoted as "without pretense to society decoration and social ambition." People who could buy more expensive furniture, on the other hand, con-

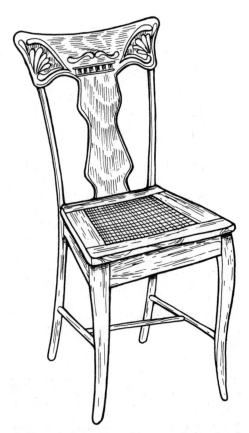

Golden oak chair with machine-pressed gingerbread.

sidered oak as being for the masses, the *hoi polloi*.

Despite the popularity of oak in its golden tones, some of it continued to be finished in the darker, traditional colors, a few of which were the following:

fumed — grayish brown
gothic — warm brown
Italian — reddish brown
Jacobean — yellowish brown
smoked — black
weathered — greenish black

An oak board displaying medullary rays. The figure is sometimes known as a *fiddleback* or *tigerstripe* pattern.

Probably the most popular color was fumed oak, which was produced by exposing the wood to ammonia vapors.

Some of what passes as oak is actually one of several other species. For a period of time practically all "oak" chairs manufactured were ash or elm, both of which are similar to oak in quality. Poplar, a lesser wood, was used in many chair seats. Chestnut, a wood that was used in many tables and bedroom furniture, is generally considered more attractive than oak, although not as strong. A discussion of each of these substitute woods is located in the furniture woods chapter.

Oak furniture was produced with much variation in its quality. One large variable was in the selection of lumber used in construction. The most favored cuts were boards of white oak often sawn to display fine interior grain patterns called *medullary rays*. Red or black oak were lesser choices, the worst grades sawn into boards with coarse, irregular-looking grain. Oak furniture also varied in its construction with cheaper pieces usually having inferior joints or veneered surfaces.

Among the identifying features of golden oak is its hardware, which is generally of two sorts. The better hardware was made from brass cast into molds and later polished. A cheaper kind was made from thin sheets of brass simply stamped into decorative patterns by machine. The two different types will be shown in "Hardware" in chapter 9.

Bamboo Furniture (1880–1900)

The use of bamboo began in the mid 1800s, but had to wait until the end of the century to become stylish. Once it did become popular, bamboo furniture was not

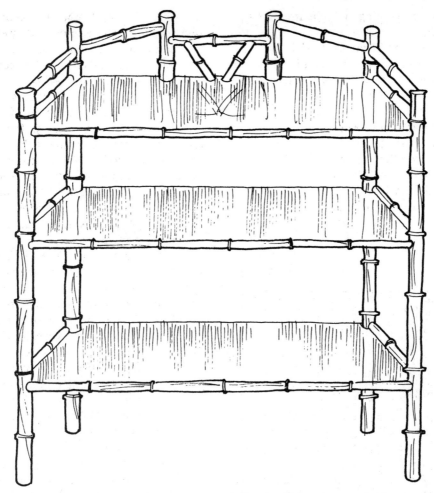

A "bamboo" bookshelf made of purposely distorted maple. Boards with a woven cane matting were often substituted for the glass shelves.

always made of bamboo. After it was recognized that the hollow tubes of the material could not hold a glue joint adequately, maple began to be used as a substitute. To give it all the appearance of bamboo, maple was sometimes turned on a lathe in an irregular way. Some very fine furniture was made using the substitute wood.

Whichever the species, bamboo was often used in conjunction with wicker, which was woven into matting to cover flat surfaces. At other times it was gilded or painted to suit differing room decors. Some bamboo-looking furniture had been made by Chippendale and his contemporaries in the mid 1700s.

3

Furniture Styles: 1900–1945

The New Century (1900–1920)

Social Background

In its social and technical history, and also in its furniture, the period from 1900 to 1920 was one of the most dynamic ever. The Victorian era with its industrial expansion and rapid social development was a hard act to follow but the new century at least approached it and was spectacular in the number of significant events it produced. The period was marked by the following social phenomena:

Boxer Rebellion—1900
Queen Victoria's death—1901
Pure Food and Drug Act—1906
Perry found North Pole—1909
Woodrow Wilson elected—1912
Tarzan of the Apes—1914

Russian Revolution—1917
big business monopolies
big stick diplomacy
federal income tax
Wobblies (Industrial Workers of the World)
ragtime
Pancho Villa
tango, turkey trot, and grizzly bear
trench warfare, mustard gas, U-boats, liberty bonds
women's suffrage—1920
Thomas Edison

The technological events, more impressive than the social, included these:

gramophone—c. 1900
vacuum cleaner—1901
washing machine—1907
light bulb—1908

first Model T — 1908
Bakelite plastic — 1909
hearing aid — c. 1910
vitamins — 1911
long distance telephone
refrigerator — 1913
Ford's assembly line — 1914
automatic rifle — 1916
X-ray — 1916
automobile automatic starter — c. 1915
water closets

The social changes listed were only symptoms of broad developments in politics, life styles, and economics. The inventions of the period were only the outstanding tips of a very large iceberg involving material growth one would think possible only in our own decades.

In history and in furniture the early decades were a foundation of profound developments eventually reaching into our own. They, of course, had had a great dependence on the Victorian universe of social institutions and material things. The new century, although it was a reflection of earlier times, was a rebellion against Victorianism in many regards. In life style preferences, the period was one of radical change. One of the largest shifts was away from formality and toward *comfort*. Residents of the new century called it *repose*, not by any stretch of the imagination our recent "hanging loose," but a kind of informality mixed with sedateness. For the artist there was so much radical change, rebellion against the constraints of Victorianism and rebellion for rebellion's sake.

The Victorian era, though it was recognized as the period of industrial birth and great commercial expansion, with regard to household organizing had been the age of clutter. In writing it had been a time of romanticized rhetoric and moral didac-

ticism. In social structure it had also been the beginning of a pluralistic society. The fast pace of technological change had led to social confusion and eventually to a confusion in furniture styles.

One of the first labels leveled on the Victorian period was the "Hundred-Year Era of Bad Taste." Elsie De Wolfe, an important interior decorator of the new century, was passionately against Victorian furniture.

> There were many fine cabinetmakers in the early Nineteenth century, but from then until the last decade the horrors that were perpetuated have never been equaled in the history of household decorations.
>
> Elsie De Wolfe. *The House in Good Taste*. New York: Century Co., 1913, p. 263.

Ekin Wallick, another decorator, had this to say:

> We can all remember the abominable styles in house furnishing which were in vogue a decade ago. Ponderous and clumsy pieces of furniture were used, highly ornamented with cheap and poorly designed decorations of all kinds. As long as the furniture was covered with tawdry scrolls, knobs, spindles and machine carved ornamentation, it seemed to command the respect and admiration of everyone.
>
> Ekin Wallick. *The Attractive Home*. Boston: Carpenter Morton, 1916, p. 23.

Philosophy of the Home

The philosophy of the home, as suggested earlier, changed considerably in the new decades. One of the main changes was a new emphasis on the total room rather than on an accumulation of individual items. The approach, while a significant advance, was still conservative in one practical sense: "Be willing to go without rather than have a bad thing and one will grow in good taste." (Wallick, p. 9.)

The sensibilities of the new century were revealed in this passage.

> Moreover, a home should be a place to rest. All things in it should encourage peace, harmony, repose and freedom. Mental and moral poise are impossible to persons engulfed in a sea of bright colors and aggressive patterns. Nervousness is the sure price paid for overdecoration.
>
> Henry Collins Brown. *Book of Home Building and Decoration*. Garden City: Doubleday, Page, 1912, p. 33.

In line with this aesthetic outlook, surprisingly, was the idea of "a place for everything and everything in its place." The opposite had often been true in Victorian times. The most important concept in the new century's view of decoration and room arrangement was *simplicity*. Often the new concept led to austerity.

Despite the trend toward austerity, house decoration following 1900 reflected a new concern with the welfare of individuals rather than the possession of things. "Decorations should not be more interesting than the people surrounded by them." (Brown, p. 31.)

Evolution of the Parlor

About 1910 the Victorian parlor began to be emancipated to become the living room, (1910 is probably the best date for the end of the Victorian era because this change reflected a relaxation of decorum and the new attitude toward comfort.) There was also another kind of shift in emphasis. "Today we plan to give pleasure and comfort to the family, rather than the occasional guest." (William A. Vollmer, ed. *A Book of Distinctive Interiors*. New York: McBride, Nast, 1912, p. 18.)

As in any age the leading edge of change was not followed by everyone. The wealthy classes, in building new homes, incorporated the new living room but retained the parlor in the form of the drawing room. Oddly, parlors and drawing rooms are still with us today as many people prefer formality or want it in at least some aspect.

The Kitchen

The second room in the house to undergo transformation was the kitchen. Partly due to the new home economics movement (begun in the seventies) and to improvements in domestic-use equipment, the kitchen began to emphasize convenience, cleanliness, and ventilation. The ideal kitchen after about 1890 was spotlessly white enameled; yellow began to be substituted later. The Hoosier-style kitchen cabinet began to be used by homeowners not having much built-in cabinet space.

The Automobile

Probably the greatest technological influence in the new century was the automobile. The automobile made commuting over long distances possible, had tremendous impact on employment, caused highways to spread out, and liberated the previously homebound. Greater travel experience encouraged many to move to other places, especially, to the cities.

Henry Ford had begun manufacture of the Model T in 1908 and by 1914 had perfected the first *moving* assembly line. (Previously the assembly line had workers moving, not the manufactured product.)

One effect on furniture manufacture, once Ford's product became affordable, was that it required funds from the household budget that otherwise might have been spent on better furniture quality. Another effect on quality was the rising cost of both labor and raw materials. Anything not made by machine methods became a rarity and its cost was high. To a great extent Ford's assembly line was a death blow to hand craftsmanship.

Golden Oak

At the turn of the century, golden oak, as discussed previously, was reaching its highest peak. It was available in many designs, most of them having some amount of glued-on ornament or machine-produced carving and trim. The prevailing golden oak styles were eclectic versions of simplified classical or French shapes varied in size, decoration, and quality. Even with its added-on ornament it was, in its own time, considered very artistic. It continued to be advertised as a democratic style because its prices were generally affordable to the ever-increasing middle class.

Colonial Revival

With its emphasis on simplicity, the new century looked back to earlier times for its furniture. Victorian styles had largely become unfashionable by about 1915 and something offering different values was called for.

America particularly sought out its heirlooms, took a new look at its earliest designs, brought back the traditional colonial pine and maple, its Chippendale, Sheraton and Duncan Phyfe (often in reproductions turned on the lathes of Grand Rapids, Michigan) and established

the antique dealer as a source of furnishings for the middle classes instead of the agent of the wealthy connoisseur.

George Savage. *A Concise History of Interior Decoration*. New York: Grosset and Dunlap, 1966, p. 260.

Among the revived styles, either as antiques or reproductions, were the following:

Dutch and Flemish
Italian Renaissance
Spanish Renaissance
Tudor
Early Jacobean
Cromwellian
Charles II
Early American
Louis 14
William and Mary
Queen Anne
Colonial
French Regency
Louis 15
Louis 16
Chippendale
Adams
Hepplewhite
Sheraton
Federal
Duncan Phyfe
English Regency
Directoire
French Empire
American Empire
French Provincial
Biedermeier

Much of the simpler furniture that was revived was sometimes known as *quaint furniture*. The decors surrounding it were considerably simpler also. The favorite color for walls and woodwork was white;

others were pale gray, putty tan, cream, and olive drab. Decorators of the new age began to see walls as background rather than something to be decorated. Floors were often treated similarly and were frequently painted.

Very popular beginning about 1900 were screens used as decoration. Often they were covered with silk, tapestry cloth, or antiqued leather. Chaise lounges, nests of tables, day beds, and vanity dressers were introduced during the same period.

Mahogany-Finished Furniture

A kind of furniture very closely related to golden oak in the new period was mahogany-finished furniture. Some of it was Honduras mahogany; others were different related species. All of them had the same eclectic qualities as golden oak. Like golden oak, many were decorated with lion's paws and griffin claws as had been the thrones of ancient kings, who were thought to derive magical powers from them.

Borax Furniture

A broad kind of furniture introduced after 1900 was *borax* furniture. The term *borax* derived from the inferior wooden boxes containing the washing and cleaning product. The furniture was basically any items made from poor materials and presenting a big facade and a glossy finish. Borax furniture, begun at the turn of the century, is still available on today's market, often having features made of artificial wood products.

Combination Furniture

Combination furniture, begun in the teens, was another product of factory technology. Intended as a type of reproduction, the new furniture began as a modified takeoff from past styles and soon became a different creature having its own identity. Its characteristics are still common today. Combination furniture, then as now, was made by using both solid wood and veneer in a single furniture item. The practice had already been used in mixing solid oak and fine quartered oak veneers, but in the teens, while good veneers were still employed, the solid parts were from cheaper species. The veneers were used for flat sections and the solid pieces for everything else. With most combination furniture the veneers were walnut or any of several species of mahogany. The solid wood used with walnut was either red or black gum. Mahogany veneers were combined with gum or birch.

One of the important things about the solid woods that were selected, even though they were cheaper, was that they could be used to take advantage of new sprayed-on finishes that contained stain. Through an accumulation of sprayed-on coats, the solid wood parts, though naturally lighter than the walnut and mahogany veneers, could be darkened to match them. The sprayed-on finish containing stain made the color and shade the same even though the wood grain was different. The overall darkness achieved by many coats minimized even that.

Because of its having two kinds of construction, combination furniture is a special case when it comes to refinishing. For a look at some of the methods that are used, see "Refinishing Combination Furniture" near the end of chapter 7.

Some of the most ornate articles of combination furniture belonged to bedroom and dining room suites. Because they are the most dramatic and numerous, they are what many people today mean by combi-

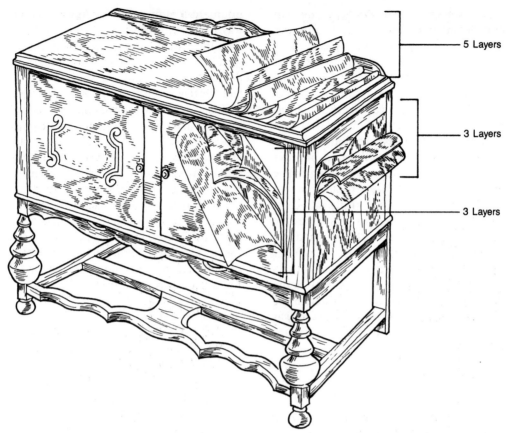

5 Layers

3 Layers

3 Layers

A combination-constructed cabinet showing its various veneer layers. Notice that alternate layers go in opposite grain directions.

nation furniture. In its broad, general sense, however, the term refers to any furniture using combination methods. It includes all kinds of stylized reproductions, however plain or fancy, however well constructed, and however apportioned in amounts of veneer and solid wood. It also includes furniture with some parts made of veneered plywood.

Dozens of manufacturers eventually produced combination furniture. The use of veneer was accepted because, at the time, most furniture shoppers did not have a strong preference for solid wood and were more fashion-conscious than anything else. The fact that it only appeared to be solid construction was a side issue with most of them. They were mainly concerned with having something new, different, or just better than they had.

Even to the skeptic who quickly saw that it could be criticized for its pretense of something finer, combination furniture could not be dismissed entirely. It was better in some ways than golden oak and its mahogany counterparts, both of which had gone downhill in quality despite their essentially solid wood ingredients. The drawer parts of some golden oak pieces were being made of poplar, a soft species that was found not to give good wear. Many parts were getting thinner, and construction methods were involving more shortcuts.

In its beginning years combination furniture was a sincere attempt to improve quality in the medium price range. The manufacturers of it were proud, and to a considerable extent, rightfully proud, of what they had achieved. In most cases the veneer used was of ample thickness and was glued together in several layers to prevent warpage. Improvements were made in several types of joints; drawers and doors both fit and worked better and were more durable. The hardware that was used was often cleverly designed and more automatic.

Art Nouveau

The first *new* furniture style to emerge in the new century was *art nouveau*. (Combination furniture was a factory method, not a style.) Art nouveau was a style with complex, florid shapes and decorations. It was a reaction to the use of machines in the late Victorian designs and a radical reaction to some of its controlled classicism.

Arts and Crafts Furniture

Another style that emerged was a diverse British creation with an emphasis on medieval motifs. Arts and crafts was highly influenced by English philosophers, especially William Morris, who began an arts and crafts revival in wallpaper, textiles, furniture, and almost everything else in the way of home furnishings.

In the way of furniture, what the movement advocated was a return to hand-produced items with simple designs and excellent craftsmanship. What emerged after two decades of the movement's functioning was furniture of many varying designs, most of them simple in shape but more aesthetic than practical. Because the furniture was handmade, it was much more expensive than factory goods and remained isolated in its production. Before it was made on a large scale it had to wait for its translation into factory versions and until the turn of the century when there was enough rebellion against Victorian styles for other styles to emerge.

Mission Furniture

Around 1900, when the arts and crafts style did emerge, it became popular along with mission furniture. The two types are similar and often confused. Today both are generally lumped together as mission, the one that sold in greater numbers. Each was usually made of oak and was basically square or rectangular in design. The difference, which is not always a dramatic one, was in arts and crafts's having touches of decoration while mission was almost completely austere. Mission became more popular largely because of its austerity. In its contrast to Victorian fanciness, it gathered much public approval.

Twenties

Social Background

As the prior two decades had been, the twenties also were a period of great social change. The word *rampant* describes it better. The twenties were, among other things, a period of fast-paced economic growth. The growth was reflected in and was a result of vastly increased consumer buying, greater industrialization, and boom-time stock market conditions. Much financial borrowing was involved in all three categories. A great flux of installment buying produced the observation that "the whole nation was on time."

The boom period, however artificial, increased consumer spending with almost all material goods. Many goods, clothing for example, were available ready-made. Sewing at home began to decrease as did virtually all handicrafts that could be purchased at a fraction of their time and material investment.

It has been estimated that 80 percent of cars were bought on time in the twenties. Many people mortgaged their houses to have them. Another estimate was that there

An arts and crafts buffet with its decorative touches.

were three times as many autos in 1929 as in 1920. Irons, washing machines, telephones, and vacuum cleaners also escalated and were bought on credit. Almost everyone had gotten ahead of himself in spending. One writer declared that thrift was dead. (*Concise History*, p. 183.)

With a prosperity that was both real and spurious, economic wealth was distributed between the middle class and wealthy magnates having immense power. Industrial workers and farmers were practically poor.

Not every advantage of the new prosperity, however distributed, was available. Many, many people did not have electricity in 1920. Great numbers continued to use gas lights or kerosene. A large proportion of the country was virtually living in Victorian times and some in almost colonial circumstances. Of the ones having a share

A mission buffet. Very little decoration.

of the new prosperity, many were super-confident and believed that science could accomplish anything.

It has been said that America went into second gear in the twenties because of the following phenomena: the speed of the auto; increased production and more mechanization; increased sales; greater population; and greater telephone communication.

The pace of life, particularly in the big cities, became a whirlwind of almost constant motion and tedium.

The New Morality

In 1920 women had raised their skirts from ankle length to 9 inches above the ground. In 1921 they raised them an inch or two higher, wore thin dresses, and even wore sleeveless gowns. By 1927 the skirt length became the knee. The automobile by mid decade had become a haven for necking and petting; drinking had become a pastime with many young flappers going "blotto" (drunk). (Reader's Digest. *Great Events of the 20th Century*. Pleasantville, N.Y.: Reader's Digest, 1977, p. 198.)

A taste for strong language had developed, and everyone wanted to be unshockable and a little shocking. There was much competition for boldness in talk, and people began to exaggerate and become loud and eventually bored. The whole period became an age of ballyhoo, fads, crazes, and heroes. Crossword puzzles, the Dempsey-Tunney fight, Rudolph Valentino, marathon dancers and flagpole sitters, the Scopes trial, Red Grange, and Charles Lindbergh received great amounts of hype in the press and in daily conversation. Everyone craved relief from the ennui produced in the new culture.

An important lesson the twenties society seemed to learn from Victorian times was not to be pretentious. Persons trying to be "real," however, took every skewed direction including glibness, provocativeness, and blatancy.

Not everyone in the twenties was involved in an excitement-boredom cycle. Primarily the new culture was for the younger generation growing up without the old values. For the young, World War I had created a disturbing crisis and a conflict with many of its elders:

. . . in the aftermath of the Great War there began a split in the national character between puritanical repression and conservatism on the one hand, and radical self-expression and profound cynicism on the other.

(*Reader's Digest Great Events*, p. 198.)

On the industrial scene in the twenties were many new, wonderful, and improved woodworking tools. On the other hand, factories developed new methods such as glue and screws to replace meshing-type joints. The old methods were often not missed by the consumer. The boom mentality of quick spending led to indiscriminate buying of furniture anyway.

Philosophy of the Home—Twenties

After about 1870 smaller houses and apartments had become more and more important. The twenties began to see them as the rule rather than something occasional. With improved transportation and new interests the home began to be less than all-encompassing. Taking on a lesser status, the home became more and more a place for relaxation, imprecision, and comfort away from an office or industrial strict regime. (Meyric R. Rogers. *American Interior Design*. New York: Bonanza, 1978, p. 88.)

The overall idea in decorating the twenties home, not much different, really, from later times, was to create a room that was comfortable as well as beautiful. *Restfulness* (the main twenties word for comfort) was very important and implied escape.

With the emphasis on restfulness, the twenties living room took on greater proportions than the parlor and was used for

A painted chair of Windsor origin. The center splat of the back is borrowed from fancy chairs made about 1830.

everyday affairs as well as the occasional visitor. For the bedroom there were two points of view. One was that it should be strictly for sleeping and storage. The other was that it should be large enough for lounging and private pursuits, hobbies and the like.

Until the late twenties the center of the living room was the fireplace or furniture organized for conversation. During the late twenties the radio became the center. During the forties the home center was the picture window; starting in the fifties it became the television.

The Kitchen

By the time of the twenties a sophistication about color had grown and white was considered too glaring for the kitchen. One popular alternative was *delft blue*—like the china of the same name. Sometimes this popular color was mixed with daffodil. The kitchen was expected to be the brightest room in the house or at least the most exciting.

Of the kitchen furniture introduced in the twenties, three kinds that became common were the white enameled steel cupboard, the porcelain-topped breakfast table, and stylized and painted Windsor chairs. Completely built-in kitchen cabinets were introduced about the same time but required more of an investment and were not as widespread.

Twenties Furniture

While the ideal in the twenties had become antiques or authentic replicas of them, the dominant furniture form in use had become combination furniture. Unfortunately, while the quality of combination pieces had been good in the teens, in the twenties it began to deteriorate.

Partly because of its bargain prices, antique furniture had become popular starting around the turn of the century. In the twenties its savings advantage was magnified by increased household spending and many people joined the bandwagon, with aesthetics ignored. It gained popularity also because of increased patriotism after World War I and a tolerance of American antiques by highbrow connoisseurs who earlier were devoted to only the European.

Combination furniture, although it was not very authentic, had grown in its acceptance by the public in the twenties. Because it was available in most furniture stores and obtainable on time payments, questions of style and quality became nonessential.

Owing to public apathy and ignorance, the construction and sale of combination furniture, much as with other designs in Victorian times, were matters of sham and deception. By the time of the twenties there had been so much stylizing, eclecticism, et cetera, that style names were becoming highly misleading. Because of the popularity of antiques the names of historic styles were taken advantage of whenever possible. In the extremes, furniture designed with but a single motif from an old style was given the name of the style to take advantage of its antique status. Pieces, for instance, with parts that were predominantly contemporary in design but having cabriole legs from the Queen Anne period were labeled Queen Anne. One of the largest ironies was the use of the label *Colonial* for furniture that was just a new version of the scroll furniture of the 1840s and '50s.

Somewhat on the same order, the stained gumwood that was introduced about 1915 was advertised as walnut or mahogany until 1926 when the Federal Trade Commission began to require honest labeling of woods, including the fact of veneers.

Borax furniture, which grew in its production in the twenties, continued to be the brunt of critics:

Where good taste is lacking we usually find highly varnished furniture of tortuous form, bedizened with vulgar applied or stamped ornament and covered with iniquitous imitation fabrics displayed against wallpaper of the tawdriest type—a very orgy of the 'cheap and nasty.'

Edward Holloway. *The Practical Book of Furnishing the Small House and Apartment.* Philadelphia: Lippincott, 1922, p. 106.

Outside the modern furniture, which was only gaining a start in the late twenties, there were no new styles in the decade, only a carryover from the teens and earlier, notably these:

arts and crafts
bentwood furniture
brass beds
Colonial
combination furniture
country furniture
golden oak
mission
rustic furniture
wicker

A few of these styles, not introduced earlier, will be discussed in the second section of this chapter.

One furniture variety that was introduced in the twenties and is sometimes considered a style was *massive furniture*. Massive furniture was combination furniture. It was called massive because several of its parts were oversized and the gross

A massive-style table emphasizing bulk. The top parts are all veneer; the bottom sections are solid.

appearance was one of bulk even though its overall dimensions were fairly normal. Massive furniture was often ornate with fancy inlaid veneer work. In the late twenties its decorations reached a baroque level and made it quite different from the simpler combination items of the teens and early twenties.

Minor Furniture Trends
in the Twenties

• The gateleg table made to go with colonial decors was big in the twenties.

• Windsor chairs for the living room as well as the kitchen were very big.

• Library tables (not necessarily made for the library) were popular beginning in the late teens. They were made in massive, Queen Anne, colonial, and other styles — usually they were combination furniture.

• Strongly built furniture was one of the ideals of the twenties. Most was massive in the ordinary sense. It appears to have evolved out of mission.

• French rococo was particularly used for the drawing or living room.

• Trunks of the twenties almost all had flat tops, which were cheaper to make than the camelback varieties.

• Half-round tables began a long popularity in the twenties.

• The Martha Washington sewing chest, built with octagonal bins, was introduced in the twenties.

• Dinette furniture was introduced for the small eating area.

• A furniture trend of the twenties hard

A massively designed porch rocker. Many of them survive because of their sturdiness.

to comprehend was the use of twin beds. It must have been the restfulness idea carried to extremes.

Decorating in the Twenties

In the twenties house decoration still sought to replace Victorian vestiges of quantification and clutter. Redecoration was having to cope with the many windows, moldings, casings, and ceiling decoration of the former times. Since a complete makeover was expensive and many people were not into decoration, the old styles persisted. Some people, on the other hand, did reduce clutter by removing the extraneous decoration that was mobile.

In decorating, the twenties were pragmatic and overly pragmatic. Harmony, simplicity, and restfulness continued as important themes and were added to by a new generation of interior decorators writing

in books and magazines. Concepts of convenience, gayness, and luminosity (in lamps and vases especially) increased the repertoire of the arts of room sprucing and renovation. Unfortunately for many people, effective decoration took a back seat to struggling hopelessly with a lot of accumulated furniture and accessories. The hoarding instinct was the primary villain.

The frequent eclecticism of an inherited decor was often not helped by popular decorators. The goal of being "smart" had become a popular one and, while it was supposed to mean knowledgeable, clever, and economical, its basic meaning all too often was merely *fashionable*. In line with this, the earlier concept of room comfort in the twenties became *casualness*.

On the positive side, the important decorator of the teens, Elsie De Wolfe, became known for emphasizing a consistent style. She was also recognized for advocating the use of *chintz* and *cretonne*, cotton materials that are still available and are usually

A half-round wall or end table. Made of gum with scalloped edges.

glazed and flowered. They were primarily used in curtains and upholstery and were the most widely used fabrics for redecoration in the twenties and thirties.

The use of color, which became very important after the emergence of interior decorators, was originally intended to achieve a relief from the times of large-print wallpapers and drab colors. When decorator books and magazines began to emphasize color, many old pieces began to be painted or reupholstered. Changing colors offered several advantages: It could bring things up to date; a single color could tie unrelated styles together; a color could subordinate texture, line, or both, or give them emphasis; and the emotional effect of furniture could be changed.

Painted furniture pieces were very widespread in the twenties, for one reason because they gave relief from having several pieces of natural wood. Painting was also considered honest compared with some other practices. At times the use of paint cavalierly ignored even a common-sense appreciation of fine woods, however. One twenties decorator had this to say:

> Woods suitable for painting, because they are hard and also have close grains, besides birch already mentioned, are white wood (poplar), mahogany, rosewood, and ebony.
>
> Emily Burbank. *Be Your Own Decorator*. New York: Dodd, Mead, 1924, p. 171.

A clever and sophisticated display of colors in the twenties was the use of *triads*. Triads were sets of deviations of the three basic colors—red, blue, and yellow. Two of the twenties triads that were more intense were plum, gray, and green, and green, orange and purple. One writer described triad combinations as humorous.

Three of many other decorating trends that occurred in the twenties were its "glue" art, which produced hundreds of simple, dainty, practical objects; a popularity of Spanish furniture and accessories; and some return to Turkish-Moorish artifacts spurred on by Rudolph Valentino's charismatic role in *The Sheik*.

Old Styles and New

One strong reaction following the teens was against mission furniture. The uncompromising straight lines were appreciated as a reaction against Victorian styles, which had served their purpose, but lacked the delicacy of period furniture. One advantage of decorating a room entirely in one period, decorators pointed out, was to add to its apparent size. On the other hand, in reaction to the Victorian, a set of matching furniture in the living room was thought to make things too commercial.

A furniture style that began in Victorian times but survived most of the critics was *wicker*. It was always valued for its informality. By the twenties, wicker was used for most kinds of furniture. It was used least for anything having drawers. Because of its construction, being woven and usually finished naturally, it wore well and seldom showed scratches.

Although most people did not distinguish between them because they were expensive, two styles of modern furniture, *modern* itself and *art deco*, became visible in the late twenties as art furniture. Years earlier they had originated in Europe as outgrowths of widespread movements in the fine arts and commercial design. Factory versions of modern styles, which began to be made here in the United States in the thirties, were often a mixture of modern and art deco and were characterized by bulk and the use of unusual veneers. Very few of them became popular until after the depression, however.

Thirties

Social Background

Above all the thirties were the depression. Following the stock market crash of October 24, 1929, 30 billion dollars invested on paper without collateral dissolved as investors sold out feverishly or could not cover their paper purchases. Over the next two or three years the gross national income dropped from 85 to 38 billion and five thousand banks closed, leaving nine million savings accounts void and without payment. (William P. Randel. *Evolution of American Taste*. New York: Crown, 1978, p. 175.)

At the height of the depression, about 1932, 25 percent of the labor force was out of work, one out of every four farms were sold for taxes, almost all private construction came to an end, and the industrial output was cut in half. By 1933 wages had dropped 60 percent for blue collar workers and 40 percent for white collar workers.

Herbert Hoover, who was president through much of the depression, was accused of lending big business money but refusing to give any to the destitute. "I am opposed to any direct or indirect government dole." Even people not hard hit by the depression lived with some fear of losing everything and having to wander like the hobos. There were one million hobos in 1932. The city dump was declared the local cafe. (*Evolution of American Taste*, p. 187.)

The economic upheaval was not the whole story of the depression. It was also a period of profound social change in other respects. Until the depression gentlemen and ladies were still the ideal and grace was important; the depression began to favor something more worldly. Human foibles had become more acceptable as the depression brought on more social awareness. There was considerable humor; it was brought on by depressing circumstances and the threat that things might get even worse.

Side by side with the depression and largely caused by it was a thirties' emphasis on recreation. "In 1935 eight percent of the national income went to recreation, the highest amount in the nation's history. The mood was psychological depression as well as economic." (*Evolution of American Taste*, p. 190.) The thirties were one of the great ages of movie-going; the talkies were in full swing and one trip to the movies per capita per week was the national average. Two other things that were important to most Americans were the radio and spectator sports.

The thirties were a great period of scientism: Science had reached great heights of popularity and for some had become a religion. Some of the thirties inventions that tended to promote a mythological view of science were:

first supermarket — 1930
fluorescent lighting — 1935
17 new plastics, including nylon and lucite
dishwasher — 1939
parquet floors
frozen foods
drycleaning
formica
aluminum (in furniture)
electric razors
washable wallpaper

Philosophy of the Home

The thirties were a time of compromise in home furnishing. They probably would have been anyway even without the depression. Houses were getting smaller and the need for furniture less. With smaller houses, combination rooms became popular in some of the same forms we have today, such as dining-living room and dining-kitchen.

Although the ideal of restfulness probably prevailed as it had in some form since the turn of the century, the theme of harmony, so popular earlier, was often at odds with *eclecticism*, the idea of mixing furniture styles and everything in the way of decoration. On mixing styles: "The subject of periods is approached very liberally now. It is even considered clever to mix periods intelligently." (Mary D. Gillies. *Popular Home Decoration*. New York: Wise and Company, 1940, p. 167.) On mixing woods: "Pine, oak, maple, and even walnut and painted furniture may be effectively combined." (Gillies, p. 168.)

Because in the thirties the public bought according to its pocketbook rather than its taste, inexpensive furniture became the mode but it was still desirable to be discriminating:

> . . . cheapness should never be permitted to be a lack of proportion or lack of design, and even more important, that cheapness should never be pretentious. Its safety is simplicity.
>
> Robert and Elizabeth Shackleton. *The Book of Antiques*. New York: Tudor, 1945, p. 189.

Furniture

During the thirties furniture was largely a luxury because of the depression. With about 25 percent of the population out of work and most of the rest having to economize even on necessities, the main approach to furniture was one of paint up, fix up, and slipcovers. Rearranging the old, rather than buying new furniture, became the first consideration in improving things. Any furniture that was purchased new usually represented hard savings or was bought by those with a relative immunity to the economic conditions.

One item of furniture that became popular was the economical studio couch. In addition to its price, it was versatile and could be used in living rooms, combination rooms, sitting rooms, and small apartments. Many studio couches were convertible. Of the wooden furniture that was purchased, the thirties was a period of increased and even more sophisticated veneer usage than the previous decade. Practically every kind of factory furniture, whether it was stylized reproductions or even modern furniture, was made in combination. The massive style, which had fairly ornate beginnings in the twenties, became even more elaborate in its veneers, some of which were imported and had bold figures. Because many of the veneers were used in overdone decorations, much of the new massive furniture was in the baroque style tradition. It was one of the most conspicuous styles since the gaudy versions of Eastlake made in the 1880's.

For a while in the thirties there was an interest in all things with a baroque or rococo flavor. It was partly a reaction to the plainness of modern furniture and other simple contemporary styles. As part of the trend, some people became interested in the more ornate Victorian designs and there was a small-scale revival of them, the French King Louis styles in particular. The revival might have taken on larger dimensions but decorators were quick to warn homemakers against taking on too much ornament and losing neatness. Although ornate antiques aroused interest, the only Victorian furniture that was revived in any great numbers was the French parlor set of the Louis 15th style.

The most popular combination furniture continuing from the twenties was stylized reproductions. Stylized reproductions, which the factories had begun to call *traditional furniture* to capture the market of moderate taste, was selling in ever-greater numbers in the thirties. Its affordability, its appeal to conservative values, and its subordinance to harmony (harmony was not completely dead) and other decorator considerations made it appealing to most buyers. (Buyers of new furniture could afford harmony; most others were stuck with an eclectic mix of existing items.)

A large amount of traditional furniture consisted of Early American pieces that were tolerably authentic and usually made of maple or pine. (Many of them, although they were made as reproductions, have been sold as original antiques over the years.) Reproductions of the eighteenth-century works of the great cabinetmakers, Chippendale, Hepplewhite, et cetera, were generally more stylized than Early American and therefore, in selling, less subject to deceit. Many of the eighteenth-century reproductions were made of mahogany of various types.

Modern furniture, which began to grow strongly in the thirties, was one of the great changes in style in the history of furniture. During the decade, modern furniture from the factories was often radical in design. Much of it had shapes from art deco, but the rest of the appearance was a dramatic one resulting from the use of striped veneers arranged in slanted patterns. The veneer patterns were, in fact, similar to the striking ones in the massive baroque style.

Zebrawood (an accurate name for one particular species) was used frequently.

In the thirties the more purely modern factory furniture was also veneered, but its shape was essentially plain. One kind (the expensive kind), used exotic veneers applied without any special effects other than a traditional mirror-matching of successive cuts of wood. The other kind, and the one that was sold in greater numbers, incorporated special finishes, especially blond ones, on oak, mahogany, and walnut.

A reproduction of an eighteenth-century highboy. It sold new for $129 in 1943.

Veneercraft dresser showing zebrawood and a triple mirror.

Art deco, which had beginnings as early as the teens, reached a peak in the thirties as factory furniture. In the twenties, in the public view, it had been the same as modern. The two styles did have similarities. Art deco was often mixed with industrial and commercial designs from the shapes of planes, trains, and cars. The mixed designs were usually referred to as *streamlining*.

The thirties, among its other accomplishments, began a period of enhanced use of upholstered furniture. A plain Turkish style brought back from Victorian times in the early twenties continued with its overstuffed bulging contours and large scroll arms. The twenties versions included upholstery made of real or imitation leather or velour. In the late thirties and for some time afterward, the emphasis was on several types of velour and *mohair*, a fabric woven from the hair of Angora goats. Because of the popularity of baroque decoration in the thirties,

some of the chairs and sofas that had earlier been plain Turkish were decorated with machine-carved moldings mounted to the front of their arm sections.

The upholstered modern furniture that began in the thirties had the Turkish bulge but had square modern outlines. Although some of it was done in a thoroughgoing modern style, most had touches of art deco, especially in the applied moldings that were counterparts of the arm treatments on baroque decorated furniture. On modern items, velour and mohair were again the main fabrics used. Some cheaper pieces had a combination of fabric and imitation leather or imitation leather alone.

Decorating

Decorating was again king in the thirties. An eclectic decor, which allowed for it, was accepted largely because it answered the problem of existing furniture. Most of the

Turkish-style sofa. Very comfortable if the bulging was not too firm.

decorators of the thirties, in response to the economic demands of the depression and its squeezing effect on the household budget, were pragmatists advocating make-do decoration and other forms of compromise.

Periods of furniture, in a compromise eclectic fashion, were more mixed beginning in the thirties. The main reasons were:

Very few could afford to throw out their old furniture.

Very few could afford to go out and buy everything of one period.

Harmony was not as desirable as it once was.

There was a greater emphasis on individual pieces.

The individual piece names, i.e., secretary, breakfront, etc., often became more important than style names.

In an effort to improve existing furniture, people in the thirties began a wide-

Modern lounge chair upholstered in patterned mohair. Fifties versions were done in nylon.

Turkish baroque lounge chair. This one is done in full regalia.

spread endeavor to refinish and renovate older furniture. Some of the effort was not always gracious. "Refinishing is all right, but the real fun begins when you start slashing furniture, cutting tables in two, and amputating legs." (Ethel Lewis. *Decorating the Home.* New York: Macmillan, 1942, p. 142.)

Accumulation

Accumulation and clutter, both of which were on the rise once simplicity began to fade, reached a new height in the thirties. Some of the items that began to be displayed were:

Audubon bird prints
framed barometers and other instruments
framed silhouettes
fruit and flower prints
glass, especially crystal

old china
original and reproduction sculpture
portraits
ships in bottles
small and large whatnots (mostly ceramic)

1940–1945

Social Background

In 1941 the American economy had improved greatly. There had been enough recovery through government welfare spending and the manufacture of defense equipment for European allies to allow the depression to wind down sharply. During 1941 furniture sales reached the highest level since before the stock market crash in 1929.

World War II, in improving the economy further, was the final end to the depression. Its production of war supplies was at an amazing rate—a greater increase in industrialization than even the last quarter of the Victorian era. It gave direct employment to seven million, and eight million more found jobs in resulting industries. The value of war production, only 8.4 billion in 1941, topped 30 billion a year later. The economy not only was recovering, it was setting new records. Farmers, the group hit hardest during the depression, saw their income triple. (*Reader's Digest Great Events*, p. 207.)

With its preoccupation with war production, America still postponed its concern with taste but continued its fascination with science and technological innovations. Here are some of the prominent inventions of the period:

A-bomb
bazookas
drive-in theaters
electric clothes dryers
garbage disposals
neon lights for home use
prefab housing
radar
sonar
standard-size kitchen cabinets
television

In 1941 a significant set of innovations for furniture factories was the invention of further new processes for improving veneer production, including the use of waterproof glue.

Philosophy of the Home

During the war period, radio and television were gaining in use and had begun to affect life styles almost as much as the automobile. One shift was away from active recreation and hobbies. Gardening, outdoor sports, crafts, sewing, and card games began a slow decline, and the spectator became a greatly increased phenomenon.

The early forties, in a continuation of themes that had been introduced in the depression, had a new sense of democracy, and one issue in furnishing a home was, according to T. H. Robsjohn-Gibbings, between wanting to live like kings and queens and living a freer, more democratic life style. An anti-antiques attitude often developed with the latter group.

Another significant matter in the forties was the old issue of just enough or too much decoration. The new industrial era and its increased wages offered considerable temptation: "We are so sure of a thousand appetites that we are in danger of passing by the amiable commonplaces." (Gladys Miller. *Your Home Decorating Guide*. New York: Grosset and Dunlap, 1941, p. 167.)

Two motives that often led to overdecorating were to liven things up and to counterbalance the amount of plain wood in a room. The following were offered by one writer as the major decorating styles that were contemporary in the forties: commonplace but comfortable, streamlined and functional, formal and dignified, and quaint and tricky. On another level the three main decors were said to be Early American, 18th century, and modern.

Kitchen

Ice boxes were still sold in the forties for folks continuing to live without electricity. The porcelain-topped kitchen table was also still available but with chromed steel legs.

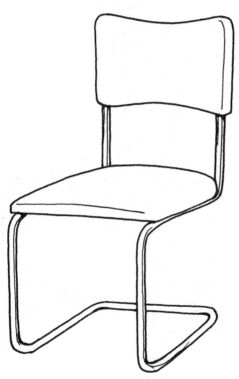

A cantilever kitchen chair made with wooden bottom and back in its early versions. This one uses plastic-covered upholstery.

Cantilever kitchen chairs of the same basic design as were made in the late twenties were probably the top seller during the period. Hoosier cabinets were still available in the forties but were virtually all painted and made of either gum or poplar.

Articles of Accumulation in the Forties

ash trays
ceramics
Chinese porcelain
cigarette boxes
lamps (too many)
pictures (too many)
pillows
plates
ruffles
small tables
Swedish glass
trophies

Furniture Trends

• Period furniture in stylized versions continued as the most popular.

• Oval tables in stylized designs were prevalent.

• Almost every style of secretary was made in the forties.

• Early American period furniture was associated with the Cape Cod house.

• A typical knee-hole desk of the forties was made of gum and mahogany veneer. The veneer was just for the top and the drawer fronts. The gum was usually stained, along with the veneer, a dark brick red. Such a desk became the business center for millions of families.

• Tiered tables in both traditional and modern styles were manufactured by the millions.

• The front porch swing, mostly made of

An early Swedish modern table. Compare with the small Shaker table in chapter 2.

Art Nouveau
(1895–1915)

The art nouveau style had its beginnings when a Frenchman, Henri Van de Velde,

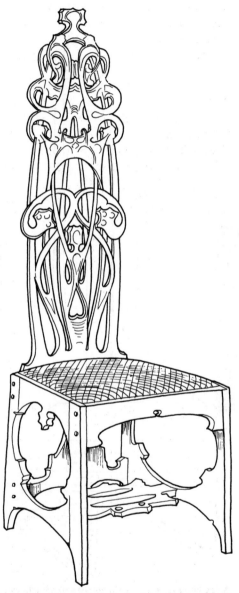

wicker or oak, remained in great use until television gained dominance in the fifties.

• Footstools and ottomans were popular.

• Cedar chests were very popular in the forties, waterfall designs especially.

• French and Italian Provincial were sold in great numbers in the forties.

• The largest shift to modern was in the forties.

• Swedish modern, introduced in the thirties, continued in popularity.

• Much of the better modern furniture was made of oak.

• Sectional furniture was a large part of forties modern.

• Many people during the thirties and forties were proud of their modern furniture. It meant a throwing off of hundreds of years of contrivance. It was largely a rebellion, an alignment with the new.

• Modern, in the forties, was primarily angular and bulky but some was rounded off to appeal to those not wanting the sharp-edged look.

• Some modern, although Americanized, was of very good quality.

An art nouveau chair created by Charles Rohlfs about 1905.

exhibited a radically new furniture design in Paris in 1895. In succeeding years other French craftsmen, notably Emile Galle and Louis Marjorelle, developed the style and gave it consistent motifs. The main motifs were the use of plant forms, especially flowers and long, undulating vines. Because of the long curves, art nouveau was sometimes called the style of the "langorous noodle." Animal forms were occasionally used, and a Japanese influence was sometimes included also.

Another branch of art nouveau, one very different from the French style, began in Scotland with Charles R. Mackintosh. His brand of furniture is sometimes differentiated as *geometric* art nouveau because of its emphasis on angular shapes. Mackintosh was not exclusively concerned with geometry, however. Much of his work was an exercise in a variety of forms. A significant difference between it and regular art nouveau was its relative absence of decoration. Mackintosh's work had a great effect on modern styles.

Although art nouveau was the first completely original style since 1830, it never became very popular because it required a hand production that few could afford. The style is included here because of its originality and because of its general impact on others. One of the few American factories to make art nouveau was the Gorham Manufacturing Company. Art nouveau's main popularity was in crafts outside of furniture. It was very popular in jewelry, graphics, sculptured glass, and metalware.

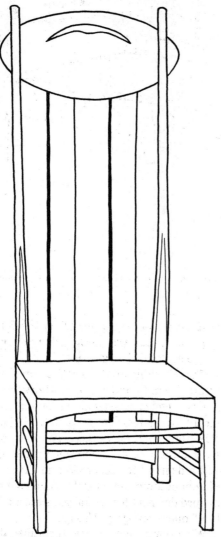

A Mackintosh chair, which was an early forerunner of modern furniture. Usually associated with arts and crafts, however.

Arts and Crafts Furniture (1900–1920)

Although this style is rarely mentioned, it was made in significant numbers and had a great influence on the development of modern furniture. It originated in the 1870s but wasn't popular until the turn of the century when it began to thrive alongside mission furniture. Much of it is similar to

An arts and crafts outdoor settee. A mission version would have a more vertical back and omit the heart motif.

mission because both had origins in the arts and crafts movement.

The arts and crafts movement, as already mentioned, developed out of the philosophy and practices of several English reformers, chiefly John Ruskin, William Morris, and Charles Eastlake. All of them were opposed to machine production and called for a resumption of handmade crafts. Their choice of furniture was not a new style, but a return to the simple, functional designs of the middle ages and renaissance.

Many of the articles constructed because of the reform movement were reproductions of the centuries-old styles. At other times they departed from the originals with designs that were simpler and styl-

ized. As was to be expected from a reform movement, there was considerable romance connected with its furniture.

The first exhibition of arts and crafts furniture was in London in 1888. Many of the pieces were experimental in design and meant for aesthetic appreciation and upper class consumption. Their very simple lines were introduced at a time when there was still a demand for fanciness and the style did not become immediately popular. It remained dormant for several years except for brief outcroppings in Europe.

When arts and crafts furniture did emerge around 1900, it was usually similar to the mission style except for having touches of decoration. At other times it was uniquely itself with simple designs and small motifs taken from medieval furniture. It is questionable how much arts and crafts furniture survives. Much of it, to the casual eye, is mistaken for mission. The difference is sometimes subtle unless you purposely look for the decorative touches.

The arts and crafts movement was the most important effort toward reforming the styles and values of Victorian furnishings. It offered new, simple alternatives to the ornateness, the pretense, and the clutter of machine-dominated articles. Because it involved several crafts of home decorating, the movement went beyond furniture in its influence with an emphasis on total room simplicity and the use of the crafts themselves. Through the attention given it in *Ladies Home Journal* and other publications, many of the movement's principles made their way into everyday discussion. Though not by itself in its influence, the arts and crafts movement was the main link connecting the styles of the middle ages and renaissance with the simplicity in contemporary furniture styles.

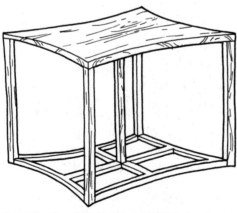

An arts and crafts table of a playful design. Probably painted originally.

Mission Furniture
(Craftsman Furniture — 1900–1920)

Mission furniture, more than anything, was a rebellion against the *machine* emphasis of the late 1800s. It stood opposed to the ornateness and rapid style changes that had then been the trend and clearly was furniture designed with a reform purpose. According to Gustav Stickley, the designer-craftsman-writer who is considered the early founder of the style, a crisis had occurred in the meaning of personal possessions. "When luxury enters in," he wrote, "and a thousand artificial requirements come to be regarded as real needs, the nation is on the brink of degeneration."

To Stickley what was needed in furniture were things very fundamental in design that were both functional and durable. In his early years he had admired the principles of honesty and sincerity set forward in the arts and crafts movement and had also been impressed by the simple austerity of the Shakers. In his own production shop in Syracuse, New York, he carried out the principles, at first using handcraft processes, and later on mixing them with those of the machine. Because Stickley's procedures were different from the thoroughgoing use of machines in the factories, he called his products *craftsman furniture*. The name was widely accepted and existed equally with the mission label.

Craftsman furniture was enormously popular during its time. During its popularity it was produced by several craft groups, including one run by two of Stickley's brothers at Fayetteville, New York. A very successful craft guild that produced the style was the Roycrofters of East Aurora, New York. Frank Lloyd Wright, it is said, grew up with craftsman furniture and adapted several of its elements in his own designs. Because of its simple features thousands of home hobbyists duplicated the style. It was one of the first types of furniture to be shown by *Popular Mechanics* magazine.

Craftsman furniture, like many other popular styles, did not remain in its pure form very long. It was quickly taken up by the factories, and millions of pieces were produced. The name *craftsman* was still used even though the furniture was being entirely made by machine. Some of the factory editions were of good quality, although in many of the chairs, the materials used were skimpy.

When shopping for craftsman furniture, one way to tell the more handmade items from the factory productions is by two style elements found in original craftsman pieces: They were usually made, in the case of seating furniture, with genuine leather upholstery, and the other element was the use of protruding, and sometimes pegged, mortise joints. The factories began to use leatherette in the upholstery and often found clever ways to fake the protruding joints.

If you find something available in this style, do not be deceived by its appearance of comfort. The chairs and sofas, even though they often have massive, square proportions that look inviting, many times were not carefully engineered for relaxation. Sometimes an extra cushion may be needed, either for the seat or back.

Early Modern

(1900–1930)

Many influences led to modern furniture. The earliest inspiration was probably the simple attractiveness of country furniture

that had largely gone unappreciated for centuries. During the last quarter of the 1800s, country furniture's simple lines and proportions began to be seen by some as a refreshing alternative to the extremes of heavily ornamented Victorian styles.

Although modern furniture was not formally introduced until it was exhibited in Paris in 1926, several craftsmen around the turn of the century had begun an evolution out of arts and crafts furniture into something distinctly different. Arthur Mackmurdo in England, Charles Mackintosh in

The peg and mortise joint in this illustration was common in arts and crafts and mission furniture.

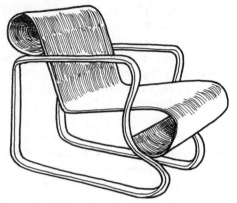

Alvar Aalto chair, made of plywood. Probably too uncomfortable to continue in wide production.

Scotland, and Will Bradley in the United States were among the early innovators.

The years surrounding the Paris exhibition in 1926 marked a full departure of modern furniture from anything with traditional elements. Several new types of chairs were among the first pieces to be introduced. The main kinds were those with chrome-plated tubular steel frames (Marcel Breuer, Max Stam, originators, 1928), those of curved plywood (Alvar Aalto, 1934), and some of chromed bar steel (Mies van der Rohe, 1929). Leather was used with many of the chairs for upholstery.

Early modern furniture was almost entirely art furniture. It was made for exhibition, for wealthy clients, or for the private pleasure of its builders. Germany and some of its neighboring countries are usually credited with its origin. A considerable amount of custom-made furniture was developed in those countries years before any production in American factories.

A significant influence on modern furniture came from abstract modern art, especially *cubism*. The rectilinear shapes of cubism were frequently translated almost directly into furniture designs. Modern art's general idea of reducing things to their simplest form was one many furniture designers found sympathetic.

Another large influence on modern styling ironically came from new industrial developments. It happened when designers began to realize that the machine and its products had capabilities beyond the Victorian uses of increasing production or creating variations on themes. Chief among the potentials recognized were the new industrial materials and the new shapes they permitted. Those who delighted in the new possibilities were often inspired by the idea of the machine itself and sought to symbolize it in some of their designs.

A preoccupation with shapes was a main element in the design of modern furniture. It began with early craftsmen interested in perfecting furniture *form* rather than decoration. The emphasis on formal beauty went further in modern furniture than a traditional concern with well-proportioned dimensions. It became a matter of achieving graceful lines and contours and appealing light reflections. A greater emphasis on

This modern table emphasized beauty of form rather than decoration. Probably painted originally. Made from plastic today.

materials and textures resulted because of the lack of concern with decoration.

The functionalism in modern furniture was another of its principal characteristics. The expression of it developed from the idea that the design of things should follow strictly from their use. "Form follows function" was the popular cliché.

Because of its emphasis on furniture dimensions (table height, drawer space, seating measures, etc.), functionalism led to a more practical way of designing furniture. Rarely was it carried out completely, however. It was usually combined with considerations of formal beauty and other aesthetic matters.

An important consequence of the development of modern furniture was a radical emphasis on the total room rather than the accent given to individual pieces by traditional forms of decoration. With the most purely modern pieces there were no carvings or inlay, very few trim moldings, and little else in the way of decorative detail. Harmonizing furniture with ceilings, walls, floors, and accessories became the most important goal in creating a modern decor. Maximizing space was also essential, and there was a tendency to lowness in individual items as one way of achieving it.

Massive Furniture
(1920–1940)

There are two important meanings for the word *massive*. One relates to any furniture that was made in large proportions for Victorian and otherwise large houses. This general massive was produced in several styles, especially mission and the revived pillar and scroll furniture called *Colonial*. Sometimes only the individual features of pieces were massive, not their overall sizes. Although frequently it was an illusion, such pieces had the appeal of seeming more durable and comfortable.

Massive furniture in a more specific meaning was a group of centuries-old styles, all having bulk in common, which were revived in vast numbers in the twenties and thirties. Their revival, because it was a factory undertaking, was in highly stylized forms having little of the detail of the originals. The times of most of the original styles were in the sixteenth and seventeenth centuries. Most of them were English, Italian, or Spanish.

The main key to identifying massive furniture is the presence of large ball turnings on its oversize legs. The ball turnings were sometimes also incorporated in stretchers connecting the legs. Outside of this feature and an overall appearance of bulk, the massive style is like much other combination furniture. It too has several kinds of veneer and other applied decorations.

In the late twenties massive furniture began evolving into more ornate forms. In the thirties it became a baroque style with an emphasis on large, curved moldings and graphic designs achieved through *marquetry* (a craft involving a decorative use of veneers). A somewhat sophisticated veneercraft was at its peak with the thirties baroque.

The most elaborate uses of veneer were to create patterns modeled after stained glass. Some of the patterns were of good design and have made the furniture highly desirable.

Almost all of the massive furniture, baroque and otherwise, was in the form of either dining room or bedroom suites. Some of the baroque dressers have triple-framed mirrors with etched glass.

For information on refinishing the massive style and other combination furniture, see the last section in chapter 7.

A massive buffet with its oversized motifs.

Art Deco
(1920–1945)

One of the major forces in the beginning of this style was the *geometric* art nouveau begun by Charles Mackintosh, the Scottish designer. Like modern furniture, art deco was also influenced by the cubist school of modern art and modern commercial design in general. The geometric influence in art deco art furniture can be seen in its linear emphasis, its angular shapes, and sometimes in a striking display of colors. The main feature that distinguishes it in factory furniture is the presence of restrained curves, particularly in rounded corners. The use of a tiered

pyramid motif taken from Aztec temples is also common. The Aztec shape, incidentally, was a major motif in art deco-designed skyscrapers, about 150 of which were built in New York City by 1945.

Despite what has already been said, art deco is sometimes difficult to distinguish from modern furniture. The two styles have in common a basic plainness and a functional appearance that contrast sharply with all previous styles. The main difference between them is that art deco, like arts and crafts, always has some element of decoration, if only in having rounded corners or a tiered progression. Because it has an overall regularity and controlled touches of decoration, art deco is often considered a classical style.

Much of the art deco factory furniture that was sold in the twenties and thirties was upholstered and made in two- or three-piece sets for the living room. Much of it had a great amount of bulk and some was truly comfortable. One of the favorite fabrics used in the upholstery was the mohair mentioned earlier in the thirties section. Some upholstered art deco, if it is in good condition, is relatively easy to reupholster because of its simple shapes.

There were two types of veneer furniture made in art deco designs. The most frequent was furniture made with plain veneer and the art deco themes expressed in the overall shape. Art deco radio cabinets with tiered sides are an example that is probably familiar. The other type of veneer furniture was of the marquetry variety mentioned with massive furniture. With it, art deco designs were expressed through inlays of different woods. Two of the frequently produced motifs were the *sunburst*, a graphics design that had become popular in various forms, and tiered *skyscraper* silhouettes.

The most successful furniture with an art deco flavor was *waterfall* bedroom furniture, a style popular from the thirties to the early fifties. Large amounts of this attractive walnut veneered style are still available. There is no supply source at present, however, for missing hardware, most of which is a combination of metal and plastic.

Art deco had a tremendous appeal during its time. Because of some of its shapes it was considered the "streamlined" modern style that many associated with the thirties generation of airplanes and automobiles. To buy art deco was to be in on an exciting modern era. It was an age of great technological expansion, especially during the years surrounding World War II. In architecture art deco is considered the last great humanistic style. It is currently being revived in some major cities, especially Houston.

Middle Modern
(1930–1945)

Until about 1930 almost all modern furniture had been in the art category and was not for general sale. What will here be called *middle modern* was the mass-produced furniture that began to be made afterward. The main types of it were: kitchen furniture with chrome parts, pure modern with plain veneers, veneercraft

Stained glass baroque chest of drawers. Probably not many of these were made, but it's an enviable item.

An art deco dressing table.

modern, transitional modern having a touch of traditional motifs, and special-finish modern.

Chromed furniture for the kitchen was the earliest type of modern to be made widely in factories. Most pieces were chairs and tables, some of the better chairs being made with painted bottoms of solid wood. The tabletops usually were made of wood or porcelain-coated steel. (Later the seat and tabletop materials were to become padded plastic and Formica, respectively.) Often the chairs were made in a cantilever design begun in Germany as one of the first modern creations. Kitchen stools with chromed legs and padded plastic seats became almost a standard by the forties.

Modern furniture, in the thirties, was not as successful out of the kitchen. Some of its pure forms had square or rectangular shapes with plain veneer. A different kind had the plain shapes but, like massive and art deco, had bold veneercraft patterns. The plainness and right angles on the one hand, and bold striped veneers on the other, were a radical departure from what people were used to. Not only did many believe it was a style that would not last, but many felt it was the ultimate cheapening of things.

Great numbers of those who rejected modern for its radical qualities became reactionaries in their preference for older styles. Many furniture manufacturers of stylized reproductions began calling their goods *traditional* to take advantage of the backlash.

Not everyone was against modern, however. Of those who liked it and would buy it in its pure forms in later years, many were willing to have it in part as long as it would combine comfortably with their existing furniture. The furniture they chose was a compromise, a transition between earlier styles and modern.

The main style that satisfied the reluctant group was art deco. It had enough of a traditional look in its rounded corners and other decorative features to fit in with most combination furniture. The other compromise furniture consisted of various versions of modern with small and highly stylized motifs from the past. Sometimes the use of turned legs or the addition of small trim molding was all that was involved in adding a traditional element.

It is not surprising that many people chose a compromise furniture. Some of the boldly veneered modern that homemakers had to select from was as wild as the veneercraft baroque. It featured drawer fronts and tabletops with veneer often applied in diamond or V-shape patterns; much of the veneer was the imported zebrawood discussed earlier. Not every surface of the style was veneered, however. Like most combination furniture, some of the exposed parts were made of gum. Significant amounts of modern furniture made during the period were not wood at all, but metal with veneercraft designs painted on.

In the forties and later, the most popular form of modern was furniture with unusual finishes, especially blond. Lighter finishes, as mentioned earlier, gave furniture a smaller appearance more suitable for smaller houses. Achieving a blond finish was done in several ways: bleaching, painting, and the use of wood fillers. In refinishing blond furniture, some of the methods that were used are strippable and some are not. Beneath some of the finishes there are often fine veneers, mainly walnut and mahogany. In addition to blond, some of the other finishes were: amber walnut; limed and pickled oak; and amber, heather, tweed, and bronze mahogany.

Waterfall chest of drawers. Probably the most popular style during the middle decades. Compatible with several other styles.

A porcelain-topped table. The glasslike surface was very durable. The drawer was subdivided for silverware.

Wicker
(Continuous from 1865)

Wicker furniture began to be imported from Asian countries around 1865. It was used throughout the rest of the 1800s but did not really become popular until the turn of the century. In the next forty years it was a leading choice for stylish decoration and was, in fact, only exceeded in general use by golden oak and reproduction furniture.

Wicker, straight from the importer, was usually unfinished or finished only with a clear coating. Through the years, however, it was often repainted by its owners to conform to the prevailing fashion. Although a variety of colors were popular during the period, as a whole, the single most utilized color was white.

It is interesting that wicker had long been made in several styles, most only barely resembling domestic furniture. The fact that it was built in the Orient and was less susceptible to American dictates of taste made it different in basic design. Since it was made in several Asian locations, it provided a diversity of specific styles.

Most wicker furniture is made from *rattan*, a vinelike palm growing in different parts of Asia. *Cane* is the sliced-off outer bark of rattan. It is the same flat, polished looking material that is made into chair seats, backs, and other woven parts. *Reed*, which is rattan's inner core, is the round, fibrous material used both in furniture and in many woven baskets. The third main type of wicker is *willow*, which is the larger, smooth, round material that is light reddish brown. Cane and willow both have smooth, hard surfaces compared with reed.

Most wicker furniture consists of one of these materials wrapped around cores of solid wood or of boards covered with wicker matting. Repair of the inside parts often means having to loosen some of the covering. Internal breakage often presents clamping difficulties also.

With their smooth, hard surfaces, cane and willow are easy to strip. Because they are woven, however, they usually need to be dip-stripped to float away any lodged particles of paint. Reed, which is more fibrous and absorbing than the others, is more difficult to deal with and can present serious problems, particularly if it has been painted red, green, or black, the more penetrating paint colors.

For a comprehensive look at wicker furniture, see Richard Saunder's *Collecting and Restoring Wicker Furniture* (New York: Crown, 1976).

A veneercraft table showing different kinds of inlay work. It is doubtful that many of these survive because of the delicacy of the veneer.

Iron and Brass Beds
(1875–1940)

Iron and brass beds were popular during the last quarter of the 1800s and continued in demand through the 1930s. Most of the early versions were made in either rococo curves or in shapes that were simple and classical or both. Those that were called iron beds were usually made of steel. They were available in several colors but the standard was white. Many iron beds had decorative brass parts that made them more desirable. A process for simulating brass developed by a Frenchman, Vernis Martin, was frequently used on knobs and medallions.

A wicker chair made of reed, the major choice of material for wicker. Look-alikes were made of paper fiber.

An essentially modern chair with a perforated traditional back and a hint of cabriole legs.

Most of the *steel* beds of the thirties and forties (their appearance had changed and they had begun to be called steel by then), had tubular parts and were painted solid colors. Many others were painted to look like walnut and other woods. Some of the simulations were indicative of the high degree to which the buying public had accepted machine processes. Instead of imitating solid wood, the simulations copied decorative cuts of *veneer*. Most of the painted veneer decorations were placed on panels of sheet metal centered on both the headboard and footboards. Woven caning was another painted motif.

The brass that was used in brass beds was generally not solid but simply tubing fitted over cords of steel. The steel was needed to provide strength and reduce expense. To resist tarnishing, the exposed brass was

A fancy bed built around 1900.

coated with a type of varnish called *French lacquer* (the terms lacquer and varnish were often interchanged until about the thirties).

It is time-consuming to refinish a brass bed. Normally the old varnish has to be removed, the brass polished in several steps, and then all the surfaces recoated. Having the process done by a metal refinishing shop* is expensive. Some shops are able to make repairs that are otherwise impossible, however. Many dents can be taken out and some bent tubes can be straightened. Most shops have access to new tubes through mail order.

Reproductions
(Continuous from 1876)

Count the authentic copies of old styles and add to them all the ones that were somehow stylized, eclecticized, or interpreted and you have the majority of all the furniture that was made between 1900 and 1945. Stylized reproductions made with combination methods were the most numerous.

A movement toward reproductions had begun when antiques started to become popular around the end of the Civil War.

---

*Most metal refinishing shops call themselves metal plating shops. A few places that refinish band instruments will also do beds.

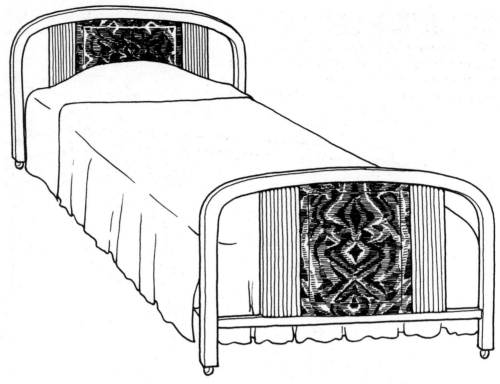

A steel bed with panels painted to resemble walnut crotch veneer.

It was accelerated by the American Centennial Exhibition that was held in Philadelphia in 1876 and the Columbian Exposition held in Chicago in 1893. Together they marked the first time that distinctively American furniture was placed on significant public display.

No sooner had American furniture been introduced in the exhibits than the word *colonial* took on large proportions. Anything that was old and seemingly native suddenly became fashionable and an object for collecting. Naturally some of what became popular included quite a lot of English furniture that had been made during the seventeeth and eighteenth centuries and shipped over to the colonies.

The popularity of antiques grew gradually in the early 1900s and then greatly accelerated in the twenties. Most of the interest was in very old colonial pieces and other period furniture made before factory goods were introduced. Because of economic factors, the interest quickly produced a great increase in the making of reproductions, authentic and otherwise.

The great majority of reproduction items made in this century are not authentic reproductions but were derived from original styles and substantially changed. Much of it was combination furniture done with veneer and machined components barely resembling anything old. It was very stylized both in the sense of being watered down and in terms of being made arbitrarily novel and fashionable.

The meaning of style itself changed with the advent of combination furniture (more so than even in Victorian times). Because the furniture was often so diluted in its motifs and so transformed otherwise by machine processes, it had only a marginal resemblance to any specific style and could only be given a general name such as Colonial, Victorian, etc. Manufacturers were quick to label their furniture with such

A Hoosier cabinet. Made kitchens much more efficient; in use for about seventy years. Probably too expensive to reproduce because of its many parts.

names to take advantage of what remaining authenticity was in them.

One of the stylized reproduction styles was *Marie Antoinette* furniture. It was popular just after the turn of the century and was basically any diluted French furniture roughly based on the Louis styles. Other diluted styles were:

Adams
Chippendale
Georgian
Hepplewhite

Jacobean or Old English
Martha Washington
Queen Anne
Renaissance

Although authenticity is lacking in stylized reproductions, the quality of construction and materials is often good, particularly in the earlier products. Sometimes the older reproductions are, in fact, much better than other comparably priced items, especially the cheaper varieties of golden oak produced about the same time. Styl-

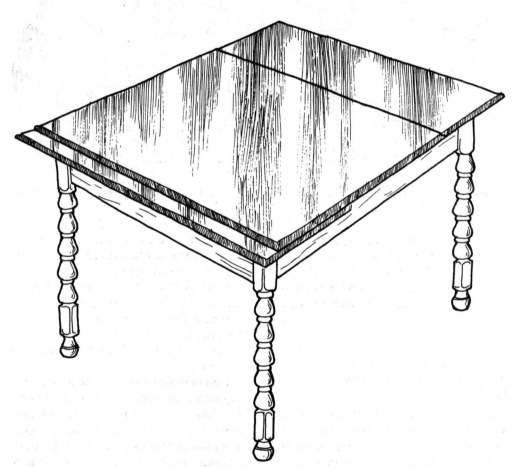

An early pull-out porcelain table.

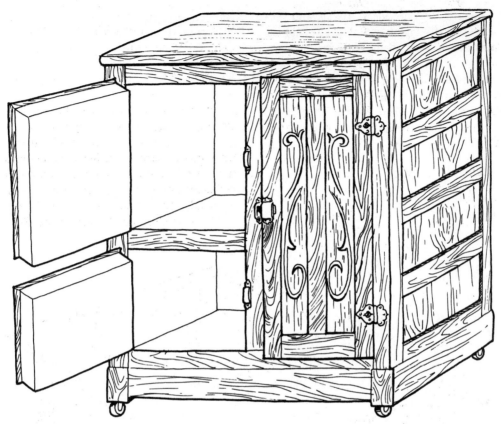

An expensive porcelain-lined ice box made around 1900. Cannot be dip-stripped because of the presence of insulation in its walls.

ized reproductions, or any type of furniture that is veneered, if it is well edged and thick enough, is, at least from a user's point of view, a better buy than furniture that has solid wood but little else to recommend it.

Hoosier Cabinets, Iceboxes, and Other Kitchen Furniture (1900–1945)

Until about 1900 the articles used for kitchen storage were hutches, simple cabinets, and built-in pantries. Tables of various types and sizes were used for work surfaces. Most things were in a category of country furniture and were handmade. Later on, but not until the late thirties, cabinets and work counters began to be built in today's modern fashion. Between 1900 and the thirties the main things in use were comprehensive kitchen cabinets designed to be highly utilitarian. In most cases they were made by the factories.

Comprehensive kitchen cabinets are today sometimes known as *Hoosier* cabinets. The name is derived from the fact that many of them were made in Indiana. One company labeled its product the "Hoosier Cabinet" and the name caught on. Others were made by the Sellers, Marsh, and Wilson companies in other states. The cabinets themselves were made in different sizes. Even the simpler ones, if they have been painted and a return to a natural finish is desired, are almost as complicated to refinish as a piano. Most of them had many components, especially the following:

built-in spice rack
glass canister set
metal bread box
metal flour bin
porcelainized pull-out tabletop
pull-out dough board
several drawers and shelves
tambour (accordion) door

Some of the earliest cabinets had bin-type drawers and were made of poplar or walnut. The later ones, which were by far the most numerous, were either made of natural oak, or of poplar or gum painted a single color, usually white. White was also used on the inside shelves of the oak cabinets. The oak cabinets are the greatest in demand and often bring a hefty price. Those with etched glass doors and those done in art deco are even more valuable.

One of the innovations of the comprehensive kitchen cabinet was its hardware. Kitchen cabinets were some of the first furniture to have door catches with built-in springs that made closing more automatic. Several types were invented. Just about all kitchen cabinets were made in two pieces: a base section with a porcelainized tabletop and an upper division containing shelves and other storage. The two were connected with brackets designed to let the tabletop be slid forward and back.

Often just the base section of the kitchen cabinets could be bought and the porcelain top used for pastries, cleaning vegetables, etc. Regular tables with porcelain tops and wooden legs were more common, however. Some of them had pull-out, spring-loaded leaves, frequently decorated with attractive designs, sometimes art deco.

Another important item of kitchen equipment was the ice box. Before the advent of gas or electric refrigerators, practically every family not having an ice house or some other outdoor facility owned one. Most ice boxes were covered with wood (generally ash, cherry, or oak) and were lined on the inside with tin, galvanized sheet metal, or, on the more expensive models, with porcelainized steel. Within the walls of each box was some type of insulation such as horsehair held together with tar or some other adhesive.

The presence of insulation makes an ice box impossible to dip-strip because of the large amounts of water absorption and the damage it can do to wood joints. Many of them are surprisingly delicate. In some instances the whole carcass can loosen and even fall apart. Hand-stripping is necessary and in this case much more efficient anyway.

4

Shopping and Buying

Shopping

Surveys done on the sale of new furniture indicate that most people buy from the first store they enter. Either they buy initially or go on to other stores and then return. Assuming the survey finding is true, and it does make sense, then it is clear that first impressions count heavily and a lot of buying is done in haste. The shopper for new furniture, while perhaps selective in his choice of stores, ends up limiting the likelihood of getting something particularly suitable by restricting his market. Moreover, if his action is consistent, he makes few actual comparisons of furniture itself.

Although more care is usually exercised, a similar trend to hasty buying undoubtedly exists with old furniture also. With it, however, the tendency to buy too quickly

is much more serious. Those shopping for old furniture who ignore the various physical problems of damage are in trouble. Those with notions that overinflate its charm and investment value but pay little attention to practical considerations like working condition, sizes, and comfort, are in big trouble.

Because it varies so much in its condition, old furniture does require careful comparison and examination. Some degree of shopping is necessary to become familiar with several furniture characteristics that are difficult to describe or illustrate. Although styles and construction features can be well illustrated, the varying detail found under real conditions can't be shown. Comparing differences in wood color; shade and texture; and things like wear, surface defects, and damage will equip the buyer with knowledge of the best and worst that can be expected. Refinishing differences and the varying conditions of "furniture in the rough" must be observed to be understood. There are large variations to be found in these respects also.

Getting Started

Some shopping around, at least until your time becomes too valuable, will give you a feel for prices. Even if you are going to haggle, you need to know something about market prices to get your money's worth. If you just want to buy one or two articles, direct comparisons between what you find in different locations is probably all you need. If, though, you are intent on furnishing several rooms or a whole house, an initial visit to several antique shops and other facilities may be necessary to develop a pricing orientation before getting down to anything specific. If you plan to go to auctions, you may want to visit antique shops and flea markets to get price perspectives first.

Price Guides

Several price guides for old furniture have come out in the past few years. Although two or three of them deal with the wide scope of Victorian furniture, the rest specialize in only one style. There seems to be nothing out at all on furniture made since about 1910.

A big problem with price guides is that inflation outdates them in a few years. Another difficulty is that often their prices are based on too small a statistical sample or one that does not take into account geographical differences—prices in large cities are higher than in small towns, for instance. Another serious problem is that

the varying condition of items is not accounted for, especially things in fair to poor condition. While most guides do attempt to present prices that are reasonably accurate and average, a small minority publish overly high figures bent on inflating the market.

Whatever their limitations, most price guides show many items of furniture, and the prices listed at least convey quality differences among the different items. These are probably the main virtues of price guides anyway.

Although some awareness of prices will be helpful, don't get hung up on something being worth such and such an amount because it says so in a book or on a price tag. Unless things are bought strictly for investment, probably the best perspective on pricing is whether an item serves your need and is affordable. Something bought on monetary worth alone may be completely impractical or unattractive.

Examining—Worth the Effort

The importance of examining old furniture will be stressed several times in this book. Because old furniture is used furniture, a thorough evaluation is needed almost by definition. The main problem in examining, however, is knowing what to look for. Since it is so important, parts of chapters 5, 6, and 7 are all concerned with it, each in different aspects.

In some cases, a systematic written comparison of articles may be helpful—it is sure to be more thorough. At the end of the general examination chapter, chapter 5, is an itemized listing of its major points. It is followed by a *furniture survey inventory* that can be photo-copied and used where helpful.

If you are shopping without much thought about style or design, consider the advantages of something with simple lines and little ornamentation. Such pieces are more adaptive to various decors and styles, with less chance for a clash. With little or no decoration, an item's color and wood grain are more prominent. Simple articles without much carving are also easier to keep clean.

Places to Buy

There are many places to buy old furniture:

antique shops
antique shows
auctions
flea markets
newspaper ads
pickers
thrift shops
used furniture stores
wholesalers
yard sales

Antique shops almost speak for themselves. Generally they have high visibility by being located near well-traveled roads and intersections. Of the various places that sell old furniture, they are the most like retail stores. Many of them having conventional hours, and a few occasionally advertise and have sales similar to those at retail stores.

Other antique shops are less conventional. In locations where zoning regulations will allow, more than you might expect are operated out of private homes in basements, garages, or outbuildings. Most of them work by appointment only and just have an on-the-spot sign for advertising. Because their advertising is limited, information about them is often only available through the grapevine. They are often worth locating, however, because of their less-commercial nature.

With the antique boom, *flea markets* have sprung up in many places. Without much convention to guide them, they have taken many shapes, everything from renovated old barns and skating rinks to well-constructed new buildings, paved and air-conditioned. There are basically two kinds of flea markets, *permanent* and *transient*. The permanent ones, although usually open just one or two days a week, can be quite large, with as many as three or four hundred dealers. Most, of course, are much smaller.

Originally the name *flea market*, which dates back thousands of years, meant a place where anything and everything could be bought, especially through barter. Many of today's permanent flea markets, in an effort to upgrade their image and reduce their customer's wanting to haggle prices, have begun calling themselves "antique malls," "antique pavilions," or something similar.

The great majority of permanent flea markets are indoors. A large building is usually marked off or partitioned into single-dealer booths. Business operations are similar to antique shops except the scale is smaller for each dealer: each one has less stock. With a smaller investment almost anyone can give it a whirl—this makes for a great diversity. Flea markets can be entertaining as well as provide a larger selection than is found in antique shops. Because of the smaller investment at flea markets, it may be, however, that antique stores have better-quality goods. The circumstances seem to vary from town to town and otherwise.

The transient flea markets, which are

most like the ancient, are usually held outdoors. Although they are only held for brief periods, one day or weekend, there may be several repetitions throughout the year. Many are held on weekends during the warmer months. Others are biweekly or monthly. A few of the larger ones are huge extravaganzas that come up but once a year.

Transient flea markets are set up in various types of locations. Open fields, drive-in theaters, and shopping malls are popular. Others are held in football stadiums and city parks. Some transient booths are often part of permanent flea markets.

Those who sell at transient flea markets may be licensed full-time dealers or just people trying to clean out their basements. The level of sales sophistication varies somewhat similarly. Because overhead is lower, items are generally cheaper.

Permanent and transient flea markets differ in several other respects:

- Transient flea markets, because of transportation limits, have far less furniture.
- At permanent markets you are in a better position to shop and then return when you have made your decision.
- Transient markets, having fewer professional dealers, have potentially more bargains.
- Permanent dealers are more accountable, have more of a reputation at stake.

Some of the larger flea markets, both permanent and transient, advertise in a weekly trade paper: *The Antique Trader*, Box 1050, Dubuque, IA 52001. *The Antique Trader* is probably the most widely circulated antiques periodical in the country. Usually it is sold on a subscription basis with about a thirty-day delay in initial mailing. Many dealers subscribe to it, and single copies may be available in some places. *The Antique Trader* covers the old furniture scene nationwide better than any other publication. In addition to having ads for flea markets, it lists many major auctions, antique shows, and wholesalers. Ads for furniture replacement parts, especially hardware, also appear in it.

Auctions, which are more fully discussed at the end of this chapter, are often the greatest source of old furniture bargains. The extra temptation to be found at auctions makes them the most unique buying experience.

Used furniture stores often have older pieces. They are a particularly good place to find twenties, thirties, and forties furniture. Prices vary considerably because of an uncertainty about whether to classify some pieces as old furniture or used.

Newspaper ads in some areas list antique furniture. The prices, since they are set mostly by nondealers (some may be dealers, however), vary considerably. Many things are overpriced, once again owing to the old furniture boom.

Pickers are individuals who acquire items for dealers. Most of them, however, will sell to anybody for convenience and enough profit. If you know a picker, you can often save significantly compared with local shop and flea market prices. Don't be surprised, though, if a picker's prices are higher. Some pick for out-of-town dealers who pay more than what can be gotten locally.

Yard sales in some areas have become so numerous that a map and a careful routing strategy may be needed for an efficient shopping of those advertised on a given weekend. Yard sales have something to offer but generally are not a good source for furniture. You may get lucky and find something at a bargain price, or you may spend a lot of time and gas just searching. Yard sales, while limited in furniture, are a good bet for the browsing shopper interested in all sorts of small items.

Thrift shops, operated by Goodwill, the Salvation Army, and many other charity groups, used to be a good place to find old furniture. Now what used to be bargains are way up in price. (The dealers got wise to the thrift shops and the thrift shops got wise to the dealers.) If you are in a position to check out thrift shops from time to time, you might find a good piece, especially in some of the shops run by smaller organizations.

Antique shows are an easy, but generally expensive way to buy old furniture. Antique shows are put on by small local clubs or by private organizers that travel from city to city. Some are held at motels and hotels, Holiday Inns especially. Most of the furniture at shows is above average quality and is usually refinished. Its higher prices result from the increased overhead involved in the dealers' travel and lodging.

Wholesalers are larger setups that sell at a discount to dealers. Some will sell to individuals and some will not. With the ones who will sell, you may still not save much except for a quantity purchase. They may be worth looking into nevertheless.

Dealer Differences and Stereotypes

Dealers differ significantly in the kinds of furniture they offer and what condition it's in. There are many shops that sell only period and country furniture, most of which is refinished. The majority of other shops, including booths at flea markets, sell a mixture of factory, country, and reproductions. Some specialize in refinished furniture; others prefer to sell it "in the rough." Some shops have one of the following as

their main line: country, primitive, oak, wicker, or Victorian.

Dealers Vary a Lot

Something that often affects a shopper's decisions is how well a dealer displays his furniture. Some seem to have a knack for making things attractive while others seem disinterested or unaware of the possibility. Dealers who are display-conscious often seek the best floor and color arrangements and may place small antiques that are for sale in and around their furniture items. Although there is probably some connection between a dealer's being particular about decorating and the quality of the furniture he sells, there is still no guarantee of good repairs, however. Repair skills are separate from a decorating interest.

The tactics of dealers who sell old furniture are more varied and often less restrained than those who sell new merchandise. In some flea markets an almost carnival atmosphere can be found with very aggressive dealers hawking their goods to passersby or quickly approaching those who stop with a ready sales pitch. Frequently they offer a lower price for any article the customer seems interested in.

In the same building, and more frequently in antique shops, the opposite end of the spectrum can be found. At this extreme may be very gentile sales methods conducted with delicate graciousness. A dealer with this style may avoid being pushy and be very nice, at least in an aesthetic sense. In contrast with the aggressive dealer who sees what he sells as raw merchandise, this one may regard his as works of art, which, of course cost more than furniture.

None of the methods employed by dealers are more subtle and powerful than the ones based on the presumption of honesty that goes with some of our stereotypes. For some people, nothing can be suspect about a little old lady or someone with a charming accent or dress. Some of the homespun selling methods used by "ordinary folks" who run a small antique store or flea market stand can be quickly captivating, no matter whether they are genuine or charade.

Not every dealer deserves this kind of cynicism. Most of them have to suffer from the minority who are unscrupulous. Those who appear nice usually are, and many are very conscientious. Many, also, can be quite frank when met with criticism. Quite a few are in the trade not only to make a living, but also to do a service by passing along quality goods at fair prices. Often these dealers do a strictly forthright business with firm prices. Even though their prices may be high, their furniture often sells for less than the gouging prices to be found in the same area.

Dealer Tactics

Discount Selling

Most dealers only appear to have firm prices. Even the ones with all the trappings of retail merchandising will probably reduce the price of a piece in some manner. For many dealers a successful tactic is *discount selling*. Except for having an advertising spread in the daily newspaper, few engage in outright sales much in the manner of department stores. Much more often some kind of privilege discount is involved, and there are reductions to dealers, collectors, repeat customers, and for quantity purchases. Discounts are usually not frowned on but are almost welcomed by many dealers. Even the simple question, "Can I get a discount?" will often bring

results. The practice is many a dealer's first line of defense against the stronger measure of haggling and can often seal a bargain.

Another type of discount can sometimes be had for a payment in cash with no receipt involved—a tax payment is thus avoided. Cash, of course, is not the sole object of every dealer, and most prefer to stay on a legitimate basis.

Naming Things

One of the widespread sales practices of many dealers is to point out furniture features that have an exaggerated or charismatic reputation. Such things as cabriole legs, brass hardware, tongue-and-groove boards, gingerbread carving, and, in fact, just about anything that can be given an interesting name, seems important to the beginning shopper whose only acquaintance may be through books or hearsay that themselves stress cliché or charismatic terms. Naming things is an important dealer tactic.

The Red Herring

Another tactic often encountered is the pointing out of a minor imperfection to obscure the detection of a larger one. A small stain on a chest of drawers may be shown, and the poor working condition of the drawers themselves never mentioned. A table scratch may be shown to draw you off the trail of a wobbly set of legs. Although this playing dumb does occur, many times the overlooking of problems is not deceit. Dealers usually do not examine their furniture the way you should when you are buying it.

Guilt and Sympathy Ploys

A few dealers almost make a living trying to get you to appreciate what they have to go through to make a living. Pleas for sympathy sometimes occur. It is not unusual for some dealers to initiate a price discussion of how the figure on the price tag is almost what they had to pay for it. Next in frequency is their having to lower the price below cost. Sometimes there's a reason given to make you feel guilty if you don't buy. A related tactic is telling you before you get a chance to make an offer that "sorry, the price on the item is wrong," but since it's his mistake, he guesses he is obligated to sell it to you at that price anyway.

Sucker Pricing

A sucker price is an extremely inflated one that is occasionally put on an item that is somehow unique or popular, or one that resembles a more costly piece. Reproductions often have such prices. Sometimes the idea of a sucker price begins with a dealer's notion of his "getting lucky." Most dealers also know that it is better to go too high than too low — it is always possible to come down in negotiations, but hard to go up. Some simply extend the logic.

Don't Jump to Conclusions

Something important that needs to be said again about dealer tactics is that some of what appears deceptive can also occur innocently. Dealers often know too little about furniture, its defects, or its prices and may say something that sounds conniving by coincidence.

Dealer Prices

Pricing Measures

There are several causes of the high variation in dealer prices. Besides the quality of the furniture for sale, the most important are location, overhead, reputation, self-confidence, and pricing wisdom. Pricing wisdom is especially important and is often difficult to come by. Ideally a dealer must set his prices well enough to bring in a reasonable profit in a desirable amount of time. His prices must provide both a good return and a good turnover. If they are too high, his turnover will be inadequate. If, on the other hand, he attempts to increase his turnover by lowering prices too much, his profits will be too slim.

Many dealers try to achieve a balance by making their prices competitive with other dealers. (To make comparisons, they often visit or send someone around to different shops in the same general area.) Others use a different method, applying a makeup figure above what they paid and making an educated guess at what a piece will bring. Although both methods are vulnerable in some manner, most pieces are appropriately priced as long as the dealers are careful and as long as the furniture is somewhat familiar. More difficulty with pricing occurs when items are out of the ordinary or are in less than good condition.

Overpricing and Underpricing

If there is no precedent for establishing a piece's worth, overpricing or underpricing can occur. Because there are more circumstances for it, overpricing occurs more often. One factor is the already mentioned dealer's awareness that he can come down in price but cannot go up. Other circumstances for overpricing include the following:

- A dealer who does not know market values may base prices on charismatic notions of worth.
- A seller may be especially fond of a particular piece and tend to hoard it by fixing a high price.
- An item may be thought to be rare.
- A seller may consider an item a good investment and will only sell at a price he thinks it will bring later.

What may appear to be a sucker price is often the result of one of these circumstances.

Another overpricing phenomenon that deserves mention is the fact that very good quality merchandise often brings prices that are disproportionately high. The reason is that better items are generally bought up faster. Quality is usually in greater demand.

Underpricing is largely the result of not knowing market values, low self-confidence, poor location, or desperation.

Bargaining and Haggling

Bargaining

Bargaining and haggling are generally expected in the antiques business even though they may not be desired or may even be frowned upon — the approach of a dealer may indicate anything but a willingness to deal. Some dealers, probably most, display a front of firm prices. Despite the front, bargaining is, for them, an everyday thing. It is normal for customers to offer a lower-than-price-tag amount. It is also normal for dealers to make out their price tags at levels that allow for bargaining.

Some dealers will not reduce prices, however. Frequently they post a sign that indicates that prices are firm. Many of them do it because they dislike the whole discounting business and the reputation that tends to go with it. Many of them feel also that their articles are high-caliber and their prices are reasonable enough. While these dealers will not bargain, others, perhaps a bit more pragmatic, give a token 5 or 10 percent discount to satisfy the customers' need to get a reduction. Still others, a large number in fact, will negotiate to much lower prices.

Haggling

Haggling, which is more contentious than bargaining, is invited by a few dealers who advertise their way of negotiating and set their prices extra-high in anticipation. Others are not at all prepared and may be shocked and angry at the outrageously low offer that is a haggling buyer's frequent opening tactic. If a dealer is willing to haggle a bit, on the other hand, what follows may include pleas for sympathy, insults, and lies and more lies. At its worst, haggling is done mainly for the sake of argument. If, instead of argument, the buyer really wants what the dealer has and haggles fairly well, he gets it reasonably and the dealer still gets a good profit. A friendly relationship may resume if both are satisfied.

The haggling dealer is at some disadvantage with some customers — the ones who assume that all dealers have 400 percent markups and the ones who tend to go overboard in insulting his character. The dealer is somewhat vulnerable if his haggling is well known: His tactics become transparent to an extent. Another disadvantage is that, despite his willingness to argue prices, he must still maintain favorable relationships in order to have repeat customers and new business. A dealer who specializes in haggling frequently tries to convince his customers that they got the best of him, or he feels especially generous, or that he wants his customers to feel satisfied.

Done with some scruples, bargaining and haggling are probably harmless. They may even have a degree of therapeutic value for someone needing to overcome being passive or gullible. If haggling seems unfair, consider the advantages the dealer has in knowing market values and bargaining tactics. Another point is that both parties have the right to say no at any time.

Auctions

A Different Structure

In many places auctions have become the chief source for old furniture. The main reasons for this are that, with an increased demand for old things, the wholesale prices confronting shop and flea market dealers have gone way up while at the same time the quantity of available items has significantly dropped. Because much of the supply of old furniture is concentrated in certain areas (a few states in the North and Midwest especially), most dealers have had to travel a considerable distance to replenish their stock. Buying the goods available, then adding the cost of transportation and other inflationary expenses, has generally meant having to have shop prices very few customers will pay.

Auctions, although their prices have generally gone up also, are structured differently. For one thing they do not have to depend on wholesale supply sources but, instead, tap the vast number of estates, businesses, and households that, for one

reason or another, decide to liquidate. One of the benefits of the way auctions are structured is that the furniture sold is fresh in the sense of not being picked over. Many things that would have been bought years ago if they had been on the regular market are becoming available for the first time through auctions. Some very fine old pieces are to be had.

For some people, especially those with an infatuation with antiques, auctions can be trouble, however. Caught up in the possibility of obtaining neat things at bargain prices and a climate that creates tension and distraction, several people at every sale go home with a number of articles that, hours or days later, turn sour. For most of them the trouble comes when things are overly idealized, poorly examined, or bid-for capriciously. More on the temptations of auctions later.

Types of Auctions

There are several types of auctions. The main division is between those that are held on the premises of the owner of the goods to be sold, and those where the goods are moved to an auction house. Another difference is between those having a central auction block where the articles are put up and those where the auctioneer moves from item to item. Some practical consequences are that with the block auction you may have to go early to get a good seat (or bring your own), while the moving auction, on the other hand, with its shifting crowd of bidders and observers, requires a frequent moving around for position.

The most numerous auctions are probably those held to liquidate households. Depending on tradition and the laws governing the settlement of estates and bankruptcy in individual states, some parts of the country have more than others. In areas where auctions have come to prevail over straight-out liquidation sales, they are often held by people who are moving away and by those wanting to make property settlements. Occasionally someone who has accumulated enough in their basement, garage, or attic may have an auction. Some household auctions are held in connection with farm liquidations. In cases where farms have been lived on a long time, there is usually a good bit of old furniture.

Moving and storage companies sometimes have auctions for storage that is either unclaimed or for which the bill is unpaid. Although the furniture at these sales is often in good condition, most of it is not very old.

Sometimes auctions that sell institutional surplus are a good source of antique furniture if the institutions are themselves old. The same can be said for businesses that liquidate.

Auction Dynamics

If you are just interested in furniture, auctions can often be boring. Most of them have a lot of other things to sell before furniture is introduced. Some people seem to be content to wait, but there is an alternative. Frequently auctioneers will accept a request to have something put up sooner than its planned order if someone has to leave early. Their reasoning is that the leaving person's involvement in the bidding can raise the price considerably. If his bid is lost, it may be very significant since usually only a few people bid on any one item. At many auctions the audience is invited to make out-of-order requests. There are other invitations to change the way

things are grouped, from by-the-pair to by-the-piece, for instance.

Most auctions are *absolute auctions*, meaning that everything must go no matter what the price it brings. A *reserve auction*, in a more guarded manner, may have the owner stipulating a minimum bid or the right to turn down any bids. Reserve stipulations must usually be spelled out in any advertising.

Something that separates auctions from most retail sales is that things are always sold *as is* unless other conditions are stated. Auctioneers are generally under no legal obligation to take items back if buyers find them to be in poor condition after the bidding. The exception is where exaggerated claims have been made. To preserve good customer relations and to be fair, some auctioneers will also allow returns in cases that are ambiguous.

Some better auctioneers, to preserve their credibility and prevent problems, are careful to examine things before a sale and report their condition as they come up for bidding. At a large auction, however, there may be little time to do this. With furniture, usually only the grossest kinds of damage are mentioned.

Auction Prices

Prices at auctions are very unpredictable. One week the mood of the audience can raise them sky high, the next week just the opposite. The weather at outdoor auctions has a sizeable effect, even if it's nothing dramatic like a cloudburst; high heat or strong winds can also thin out a crowd. Few auctions are cancelled during the course of a sale, however, and prices can go quite low. The water damage that affects furniture when there is a rain storm usually is just in the finish. There is little harm to a piece that has to be refinished anyway.

In many areas several auctions compete with each other on a given day. This has a large effect on prices and so does advertising. A newspaper ad listing many *antiques* will generally attract more customers. Some say that auctions bring higher prices at the beginning of a new season in the spring.

The most interesting thing about auctions is the excitement and anxiety many people feel. In extreme cases they amount to what might be called *auction fever*. Some semblance of it is probably felt by anyone who bids at auctions. Initially there is the thrill of getting desirable old things at cheap prices. Next enters an awareness of competition and the feeling of risk in getting carried away and bidding too high. The ingredient that usually intensifies things is the banter and tempo of the auctioneer. The loud and boring chants of most auctioneers tend to reduce concentration and lead to rash decisions. Not all of the reaction is in favor of the auctioneer, however. While some people become extravagant, others draw into a shell and resist bidding.

Runners and Phantoms

The most talked-about tactic sometimes employed by auctioneers is the use of *runners*. Very simply a runner is someone hired to bid items up in price. Sometimes the maneuver backfires and the auctioneer gets stuck with the goods. Families that are having an auction sometimes have members acting as runners. (Usually, though, they are just trying to acquire family keepsakes.)

A less-discussed tactic than the runner, but one that is probably more widespread,

is the use of the *phantom bidder*. A phantom bidder is a runner contrived by an auctioneer. The practice is made possible by the widespread use of discreet bidding. A slight nod of the head, a small finger raised, or an eyewink are all acceptable bids. Someone who suspects a phantom bid, but has no direct proof, may be forced to concede that an actual one was made in one of these subtle ways. The most dramatic (and dastardly) use of a phantom bidder is to confuse a customer with a tempo that quickly moves the bid back and forth between him and the imaginary bidder.

If you see the same furniture at an auction house in successive weeks, it could mean that runners or imaginary bidders have been used unsuccessfully. It could also mean, however, that a customer did not pick up his item, or that an honest mistake was made by the auctioneer.

High Prices and Bargains

Some people say that high prices at an auction are caused by antique dealers looking for merchandise for their own businesses. The truth is that dealers, in order to make a profit, have to keep their bids significantly below what they would charge for things in their shops. In the process they do tend to raise prices, but seldom above a wholesale level and rarely overall. Prices are raised more generally by uninformed bidders who overvalue items. On selected pieces, prices tend to go to extremes when bid on by pickers buying for dealers living in higher market areas. A similar thing happens as a result of competition among collectors bidding for rare or especially fine articles.

In spite of the different phenomena that increase prices, there are still bargains to be found at most auctions. Many of them arise as a result of an audience's makeup and mood; others are due to differing patterns of like and dislike. Most of the collectors, pickers, and other higher bidders may be away at a competing auction or planning to attend one they feel is more promising the following day. Financial matters revolving around tax time, payday at the end of the month, and the nearness of Christmas all have their effects on prices. Sometimes when these factors come together favorably a large number of bargains occur. At other times bargains come up during the lulls between high-priced items and as a result of a general confusion and hesitation.

Successful Bidding

Successful bidding, defined as getting furniture at less than antique shop or flea market prices, is possible at most auctions. Although the considerations that must be made are fairly straightlaced and stoical, they will ensure either getting furniture that is in good condition at affordable prices or getting nothing at all. (Getting nothing still belongs in the win column, because it beats paying too much for something or getting something you don't need.) There are several steps to ensure success one way or the other:

Know market values. A trip to a flea market or to antique shops will give you a general idea of what you'd have to spend outside of an auction. It will tell you what kind of value you're getting when you bid.

Know what you can afford. Set a maximum figure totally and for each piece you want to bid on.

Thoroughly inspect items. Even though no one else seems to be doing it, it is important to inspect each piece you consider with a careful scrutiny. A list of the points covered in chapter 5, "Examining Old Furniture," may be a useful reference. It is at the end of that chapter.

Estimate repair and refinishing costs. This is one of the least certain steps. One fact is that repair and refinishing work is usually underestimated. The detailed considerations in the repair and refinishing chapters will help with estimating to some extent, but the rest will depend on judgment. Be as specific as you possibly can in detailing any work that is needed. Be liberal with labor/material costs in cases where you're not sure.

Setting bidding limits. Set them low enough on each item so that if you win the bid, you'll be glad to pay the price you've set. Do not consider your figures as estimates but, rather, as *firm maximums*.

Set priorities. Decide which of the items you've considered are needed and which are just fancy. Select some alternative pieces in case you don't get your first choices during the bidding. Do any revising of figures before you get into the thick of things.

Find a comfortable place to sit or stand. Find one where you can observe the auctioneer and some of the audience. This will help you see if bids are legitimate and, to a degree, keep things honest in case they're not.

Listen carefully to the bidding. Listen to the general terms of sale at the beginning of an auction. Pay attention with each auction lot as to whether it is to be sold by the piece, by the pair, etc. Listen carefully to the bidding, both to be alert to the normal circumstances and to keep an ear open for any shady dealings. Some auctions, you'll discover, are done honestly enough so that you can let down your guard after taking initial precautions.

Bid according to your limits only. Along with a careful examination, this is one of the things most bidders find hardest. If you want to make an exception, keep your increases *strictly conservative*. You may wish to have an exact limit, such as 10 percent more than your original.

Secure your successfully bid items. In most places items that are bought at auction immediately become the responsibility of the successful bidder. The consequence is that the customer has the choice of either taking things to his vehicle or having the faith that they'll be spared the accidents, theft, and mistakes that sometimes occur during the commotion of many auctions. Furniture is actually less of a problem as long as it's heavy and bulky and takes two to carry. The furniture things that are vulnerable are small items that can be concealed and things like mirrors that are easily broken. Mistakes occur often at auctions having a lot of similar items.

Another matter for security involves keeping a running record of your purchases. Doing this gives you an account of your spending and can sometimes help solve any discrepancies with the auction's cashier.

5

Examining Old Furniture

The Need for Examination

Old furniture comes in every condition from shoddy and decaying to almost mint. Although you can occasionally find items in prime condition, most things have received some amount of wear or damage that will require repair measures. For a piece to need no work is rare, especially if it is complex in design, has moving parts, or was meant for practical use. Even furniture that is already refinished needs attention. Much of it, for reasons of lack of know-how or expediency, has been redone superficially. While the beauty of the wood may be obscured by a dull and darkened finish in an unrestored piece, it may be misleadingly highlighted in one that has been done over quickly.

Because of a frequent need for repair and refinishing work, a careful examination of old furniture is indispensable. There is no alternative for it in knowing periods and styles, becoming knowledgeable about prices, or in relying on an item's outward appearance, however appealing. Even though an examination is the best measure for ensuring value, most people only inspect old furniture in one or two aspects and then usually from a distance. One reason for the superficial approach is not wanting to offend the seller.

In most cases the greatest variation in the monetary value of old furniture is determined by its condition. The cost of an item in good shape may be only a few dollars more than a similar one needing lots of work, yet it is not at all unusual for the cost of repairing and refinishing the lesser piece to mount up to two or three times more.

Those who sell furniture in need of more than a little work often underestimate the time and costs involved. Their prices usually are not low enough to compensate for the work needed, and getting them to see reason is often impossible. A few sellers presumably know what's involved in such repairs, but set their prices in anticipation of the buyer who doesn't.

Not Gracious but Necessary

As necessary as it is, examining old furniture is not a gracious undertaking. It requires a good measure of skepticism, looking high and low, inside, outside, and sideways, trying out moving parts, and measuring dimensions for practical use.

The aim of this and some later chapters is to help you examine furniture well enough to know the work it may need, to prevent the misfortune of buying what is impractical or impossible to fix, and to ensure getting good value. In this chapter the points of examination to be discussed are general ones referring to a variety of furniture items, especially items "in the rough." Information about already refinished articles is near the end of this chapter. Other information, arranged according to particular types of furniture, such as beds or chairs, will be taken up in chapter 6, "Repair and Usage Considerations." Examination matters that relate to refinishing will be taken up in chapter 7, "Refinishing Considerations."

A Physical Inspection

Most items of furniture have many individual sections and parts. To avoid missing some in an inspection a systematic approach is needed. With many pieces you may wish to use an approach based on the notion that most things have seven sides (including the inside). A different method would be needed, of course, for a round pedestal table or anything with an irregular shape.

The Lighting Matters

Although it may uncover unpleasing flaws, it is best to examine furniture in adequate light. To curb overhead, many antique stores and flea markets are dimly lit. In some situations it may be appropriate to ask to carry the piece you are examining to a better light source, even outdoors. In other cases the only thing practical may be a strong flashlight. A flashlight is probably the single most helpful tool to take when shopping for furniture. Be careful of appraising the color of furniture as it appears under artificial lighting. Some bulbs, either fluorescent or regular, make things appear unnaturally red.

All Parts, Right Parts

Once you have the furniture in good light, make sure it is complete. In order to display tables in their more convenient and attractive smaller sizes, many dealers store the leaves elsewhere. Other parts may be stored separately for convenience but are sometimes simply misplaced. Missing parts are usually very important. Don't get talked into believing that a missing fifth leg is not an integral part of a leaf table or that table leaves are inexpensive to have made. After locating a stray part, it is equally important to make sure it fits. Most similar-looking parts are not interchangeable.

Another kind of important part is the broken-off piece that needs to be glued back in place. Not having one of these when repair time comes can lead to considerable expense. If an item has drawers, the missing piece may be in one of them. If it cannot be found, the purchase price should be reduced to compensate for the cost of replacement and the lowering of the piece's value.

Moving Parts, Loose Joints

Moving parts are crucial in an examination. Drawers, doors, table slides, and anything else that tracks or hinges all need attention. Often they are complex and expensive to repair. At other times, with a little know-how, you can fix them with surprising ease. Information about furniture with moving parts is presented in chapter 6, "Repair and Usage Considerations."

Some old furniture may be dilapidated due to glue deterioration in its joints. The arms of a rocking chair or some of the drawer fronts of a desk may have come off. Replacing these pieces basically involves scraping away the old glue, then putting them back with fresh glue and clamps. If the loose parts are connected to others that are affected, the time involved can especially mount up. A domino effect on adjacent parts often occurs. The best way to determine looseness is to wobble a piece and pry by hand against any parts that are in question. Because chair parts receive extra stress, even a slight looseness in them should be treated as significant since it can lead to eventual breakage.

Alignment and Stance

The alignment and stance (touching the floor with all feet) of a furniture item are important. Repairs to a misaligned piece, if there are several parts involved, can require a number of clamps, some basic car-

pentry knowledge, and some very careful work. However out of whack a piece may be, it is a fair assumption that it originally was made with an even stance and with level and square parts. If an article has a good deal of looseness, it can probably be returned to its proper condition if repairs are done well. Pieces that hold together tightly, but still have an alignment problem, may have been improperly repaired previously and may need to be dismantled and the work done over.

Evenness of legs, a factor as necessary for keeping a piece sound as it is for appearance, is often difficult to assess because of the unlevel floors in some dealer's shops. Without a level floor you may have to resort to other means. Check for wear on leg ends, and make sure legs themselves are equal in length. Leg ends frequently decay due to dry rot and are susceptible to rough handling.

Repair efforts to equalize the length of legs have many times only made things worse. Any small differences that might be noticed can easily be remedied by methods discussed under "Chairs" in chapter 6. Other aspects of levelness besides leg length are discussed under "Tables" in the same chapter. Matters of squareness are commonly judged by sight and comparison. A small square or anything known to be square might be helpful with some articles.

Sturdiness

Anything that bears weight or has moving parts must be sturdy. Sufficient structural supports and adequate joints are necessary, and the wood used, preferably hard and strong, should be of ample thickness. Despite the need for it, sturdiness was often sacrificed in the several styles having an emphasis on elegance of form with trim lines. Most of them feature delicate curves and legs. Other furniture, by contrast, may have a high degree of sturdiness accomplished by mere bulk. Some, but not all mission furniture is in this category.

The View Down Under

Looking under a furniture item can usually tell you something about its quality and condition; the raw, unfinished parts are more easily judged and can confirm problems noticed on the exterior. The lower underneath part of a cabinet is critical in terms of water damage and warpage. Dry rot and termite damage are more likely to be found on and around its bottom shelf. Many old repairs are visible from underneath furniture. Sometimes they continue as trouble spots and need further work.

Wear vs. Damage

Surface damage is an important matter. One type, the wear that occurs with the normal rubbing and abrasion of years of use, is generally considered acceptable if it is not too extreme. Rounded edges and corners are common. Their presence often adds character through their softening effect. Old cupboards with a succession of circular markings left by the moving of their turn latches once the old positions had worn too deep have extra charm.

Marking, another kind of wear, consists of the small dents and other impressions made in the wood by daily use. It is found on almost all old furniture and is probably the most prevalent kind of wear. Other kinds of surface damage may convey more than normal use. The dents and bruises caused by rough use or handling accidents vary considerably in their severity and number. Very old country furniture and anything made with a soft wood such as pine or poplar can be expected to have a full share of dents and bruises. Finer and more recent furniture should ideally have little.

Holes, Gouges, and Cracks

The usual method for dealing with holes, gouges, and cracks is plastic wood. Unfortunately, used right out of the can it seldom matches the surrounding wood and stain must be mixed with it. The problem is lessened with some of the newer wood fillers, those with a real plastic base rather than cellulose. Because they come in a variety of colors to begin with, and also take stain easily, they eliminate some of the trial and error.

The putty or wax sticks primarily intended for paneling and millwork are usually too soft for furniture. The professional treatment for ordinary holes and gouges is the use of shellac sticks or lacquer sticks that come in a great variety of colors. These sticks are melted into the damaged area and then leveled to conform with the surrounding surface.

Most cracks can be closed with the use of glue and clamps, but any dirt must be cleaned out carefully without scarring the edges. Some cracks, unfortunately, are too wide to close and must be repaired with a carefully cut wedge.

Cleaning May Suffice

Although most old furniture needs refinishing, some of it can get by with just a good cleaning. Whether a piece just needs cleaning is easy to determine if the old finish is visible and has no crackling (alligator effect) or other type of deterioration.

An old cupboard with a succession of circular markings created by the moving of its latch.

Cleaning in such a situation may be accomplished with a rag and *mineral spirits*, a type of paint thinner usually sold in bulk under the name of *Varsol*. If a piece has considerable surface dirt, however, the condition of both its wood and its finish are obscured and some amount of cleaning is needed just to see if cleaning will suffice. Because any hidden places of bare wood will absorb the dirt in a liquid cleaning procedure, a brush or dry rag is preferred if bare places are in evidence. Dirt that has already gotten into the wood, if it is significant, is a serious problem with no completely satisfactory solution.

The Nose Decides

Smelling the furniture is a way to screen out certain bad odors. The problem occasionally comes with old kitchen pieces. Some of them were used to store meat and other foods, the residues of which became imbedded in the wood and turned rancid. Some of these smells are very difficult to remove without the use of dip-stripping.

Stains and Burns

Any stains that were caused by accidental spilling should be located and identified, if possible, during an examination.

Some of them cannot be removed. See the section on surface preparation in chapter 7, "Refinishing Considerations," for a longer discussion about them.

Burns are a difficult problem to correct. With the usual solution of scraping away the char, some of the wood is lost and a noticeable depression remains. With small burns a plug cutter can sometimes be used to make a patch for the affected spot. Large burns, on the other hand, may require the replacement of a whole section. For quick results many burns are covered with a vase or doily.

Types of Decay

Some old furniture may have damage done by dry rot, boring insects, or termites. Sometimes the damage is more extensive than it appears on the surface. Tapping around the visible damage may help determine its limits. A better indication may be had by probing with wires or pins. Some

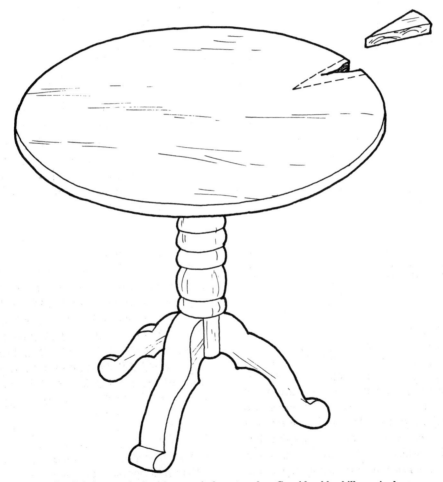

Crack being repaired with a precisely cut wedge. Considerable skill required.

say the presence of wood dust is evidence of live insects. Whether it is insects or just residue from their former occupancy, precaution is needed to be certain that further damage is prevented. If a piece is going to be dip-stripped, the tank chemicals will do the job. Some types of home fumigation will also work.

Contrasts in the Wood

Some furniture contains light strips of wood that contrast with its predominant color. Usually this is *sapwood* that was included to save money in manufacturing. If a piece containing sapwood is going to be refinished, the patches of it can sometimes be stained to match the main color. The job is usually done carefully with an artist's brush.

Another kind of contrast happens when furniture parts have been bleached by sunlight. The problem often occurs when furniture is placed in front of or in line with direct light from a window. Sometimes the bleaching covers a large portion of a piece, or it may occur when just a peephole of light comes through a windowshade or blinds. Making sunlight indirect by the use of sheer curtains is one good way to prevent such problems and, to some degree, can help minimize existing ones over time.

Tests

Much of the old furniture you will encounter needs refinishing. Whether or not you are experienced in doing the work, some means are needed to help diagnose an existing finish and give a good idea of the results to be had with a new one. Some practical tests can help. Scraping off a small area on a painted article has become a widespread practice for determining the number of coats of paint and the kind of wood underneath. If care is not taken, though, some of the wood is scraped away and a spot that is conspicuous may result after refinishing. Pieces that are stained should never be scraped. In cases where scraping is safe, the preferred method is to work on a small, obscure area with a dull knife having a curved blade. The curved blade helps prevent nicks and gouging. In detecting just the kind of wood, scraping can usually be avoided by checking places like the backs of drawer fronts, the up-and-under parts of legs, and the underside of tables.

Test for Strippability

Another test, one which more directly assesses the strippability of an old finish, involves the use of paint and varnish remover. The test is not especially popular with dealers, but it is the best method for predicting the level of difficulty in both hand and dip-stripping and detects the few cases of finishes that cannot be stripped by either. If you are experienced in recognizing old finishes, you will not need to use the test for those that are easily stripped and will be able to reserve it for those that are questionable. You will almost always find it useful for assessing several layers of old paint.

The test begins with the sometimes difficult task of getting the dealer's permission. Many will agree if the piece clearly needs refinishing and if they know you are seriously interested. A kit for the test consists of:

• A small amount of paint and varnish remover. Use the type made of *methyline chloride* whithout any toluol or acetone.

The last two ingredients are found only in the cheaper grades.

- A brush or something else to apply the remover.
- A paint scraper to "lift" the softened finish.
- Number 2 or 3 steel wool to further remove it.
- Newspaper to prevent spills.

The remover should be blobbed onto a horizontal spot if possible. Blob on plenty and wait ten minutes (more if you must work vertically). Next comes the steel wool to clean up the remover and softened finish. In many cases all of the finish will be removed and a favorable prediction for stripping the entire piece can be made. Results that are less than complete mean harder work. Repeated applications may be needed to determine how hard. A very small number of old finishes may scarcely be budged by the test and may need to be removed by very prolonged and repeated applications or by scraping with a curved, dull knife. The scraping method is only safe with the harder woods, however.

Painted Furniture

One test of strippability or another is especially needed for articles that are painted. Stripping paint is often time-consuming and tedious. It is especially difficult when there are many coats, when there are many grooves and crevices to clean, or when the paint is on bare wood that has open pores (like oak and walnut). Red, green, and black paint are very difficult to remove from bare wood. These colors seem to have an extra penetrating quality. Although all painted furniture should be skeptically considered because of the possibility of hidden surface damage, stripping itself can be relatively easy when there is a coat of shellac under the paint.

Shellac

Shellac is, in general, the easiest old finish to remove. It was the *clear* finish used on old furniture over 90 percent of the time. Except on walnut and other naturally dark woods, shellac is perfect for dip-stripping. It comes off fast and, unlike paint, very little of it remains in grooves and crevices. With hand stripping, shellac will also come off easily unless it is very thick. Even so it is still below paint in stubbornness.

Stained Furniture

Even though shellac is classified as a clear finish, it was often used in conjunction with stain. Either the wood itself was stained and the shellac added afterward, or the stain was included with the shellac. Distinguishing the two types is difficult without some sort of test, and there is a significant difference when it comes to stripping. Stain in the wood can be only partially removed, while shellac-stain is almost entirely removable. Lacquer and varnish, finishes that began to be used around the twenties, are removable about like shellac. Almost any clear finish, then, is easy to remove compared to several layers of paint.

Most of the staining done on old furniture was an attempt to make an inexpensive wood look like cherry, mahogany, or walnut, the woods prized for their outstanding colors and woodworking ease. Some of the stained articles you'll encounter may be fine imitations and look good in their own right. If you want to be sure, though, that you're getting one of the prized woods, many comparisons of them and their imitators may be necessary. Consider the following:

Prized Woods	Imitators
cherry	birch, maple, poplar
mahogany	birch, gum, cheaper mahoganies
walnut	birch, gum, poplar, pine

Chapter 8, "Furniture Woods," contains information for making several comparisons.

Already Refinished Furniture

Much of the furniture that is for sale on today's market is already refinished. The quality of the work, of course, varies considerably. On one end of the spectrum are pieces done with a great deal of skill and care; on the other are those with one slapped-on coat over a rough texture of raised grain or sanding marks left behind by the refinisher. Several other kinds of poor workmanship often show up.

Although they may appear attractive from a distance, some pieces can be found to have considerable dust in the finish. Paint left over from stripping may appear in cracks and crevices or may be in the grain of the wood itself.

You may well want to avoid furniture that has its *patina* sanded away. Patina is the naturally aged surface layer of wood that gives old furniture much of its charm. Wood that has none lacks luster and is generally lighter in color. It looks like new wood. Table, desk, and dresser tops are frequently deeply sanded to remove accidental stains, and the patina is removed in the process.

Many pieces of refinished furniture, especially those made of oak, have a slightly dark, washed-out appearance that results from the incomplete stripping of a dark penetrating stain. Often there is a slight grayish cast, occasionally a green. Oak was stained several more colors than golden yellow. Dealers do not usually restain such pieces because to do so would darken them. They leave them unstained because, even washed out, they resemble the more popular and saleable lightness of golden oak more than if any kind of color was added.

Be cautious of finishes that are tacky. The condition usually results from applying a varnish when there is too much moisture in the air. A tacky finish may dry eventually but may deteriorate quickly.

To do an ordinarily acceptable job of resisting water and other spills, a finish must be sufficiently thick. Most manufacturers recommend a bare minimum of two coats just to achieve a level of protection they term *water resistant*. You can improve your chances of getting this level by comparing several refinishing jobs to see what thicker finishes look like. Complete waterproofing can only be achieved with sufficient coats of polyurethane or other varnishes. Any furniture likely to receive frequent spills needs such protection.

Furniture that is refinished well with a soft luster of sufficiently thick varnish or other material must still be critically examined for repair needs. A dealer who is selling a piece may have discovered the need for repairs only after buying it and decided to forego them to maintain a needed profit level. With some dealers, especially those doing a brisk business, the need for some types of small repairs may go unnoticed entirely.

Stripped Furniture

In some areas of the country *stripped furniture* has become popular. Most of it is in the golden oak category. Pieces needing to be refinished are dip-stripped and then either sold as is or with some repair and refinishing steps taken. Often they are sold from the backs of trucks, in temporary warehouses, or in other circumstances that do not invite close inspection. However clean and conducive to optimism such pieces may appear, they, too, are still subject to most of the problems already discussed.

Veneered Furniture

Although most people prefer solid wood, veneer has some definite advantages and was used in some very exquisite furniture. One advantage of veneer is its resistance to warpage. It is made possible because the grain of succeeding layers is laid in opposite directions, each counteracting any distortion to the next. Another benefit of veneer is the use of woods that would be too expensive or fragile in solid wood form. Burl walnut, for instance, breaks easily as solid wood.

Veneer, of course, also has its disadvantages. Often the glue holding it in place fails. Bubbles resulting from its loosening sometimes form in the middle of larger flat sections, while narrow pieces of veneer glued to edges are very vulnerable to anything but delicate handling. To repair damaged interior veneer in an exacting way requires special tools and the right wood thicknesses for replacement. Almost all of today's replacement veneer, unfortunately, is much thinner than that used on old furniture.* Most repairs require either using old veneer or gluing two or more new thicknesses together.

Veneer can be detected in several ways. Usually its thin layer is obvious along board edges. Its existence is confirmed where there is a difference between a board's top surface grain patterns and those of its ends. Fancy figures such as burl and crotch are almost always veneer. Some matched sections of fancy veneer consist of consecutively sliced cuts of wood arranged as opposite images of each other. This is the *mirror matching* mentioned in chapter 3.

---

*Much veneer that began to be used in the thirties was also very thin.

Inspection Checklist

____ Seven sides inspection.
____ Adequate light.
____ Are all the parts there?
____ Are broken-off pieces on hand?
____ Do moving parts work smoothly?
____ Are any parts loose?
____ Are parts in their proper alignment?
____ Does the piece have its proper stance?
____ Is floor level?
____ Are leg ends intact?
____ Are doors and other parts square that need to be?
____ Is piece sufficiently sturdy for its function?
____ Are lower portions free from dry rot or termites?
____ Are there serious dents, gashes, or cracks?
____ Will a good cleaning suffice?
____ Any really bad smells (a slight musty odor is normal)?
____ Any stains from accidental spilling?
____ Are there any deep burns?
____ Is there any sapwood?
____ Any severe contrasts caused by sunlight bleaching?
____ Paint scraping test to decide number of coats and colors.
____ Paint and varnish remover test.
____ Is the piece painted red, green, or black?
____ If a piece is stained, is the color in the wood or merely in the finish?
____ Does a refinished piece have dust in the finish?
____ Has the patina been sanded away?
____ Does the piece have an unattractive washed-out appearance?
____ Is the finish tacky?
____ Does the finish appear to be sufficiently thick on a piece that needs it, such as a kitchen table?
____ Any missing veneer?
____ Does the piece have all its hardware?

Old Furniture Evaluation Inventory

Item Description _____

Location _____

Kind of Wood _____ Solid _____ Veneered _____

Damage, Missing Parts, or Hardware:

Description	Est. Cost or Time Involved	Comments
_____	_____	_____
_____	_____	_____

Practical Dimensions:

___ height   ___ diameter   ___ vertical back

___ length   ___ seat height   ___ slant back

___ depth or width ___ leg room   ___ (   )

Mattress size needed _____

Shelf or drawer sizes _____

Finish*:

___ original finish (clear or combined with stain)

___ original finish over stain in the wood

___ varnish stain over original finish

___ paint over bare wood; approx. no. of coats ___

___ paint over shellac; approx. no. of coats ___

___ unstrippable, except by scraping

Condition of Finish*:

___ usable as is

___ just needs cleaning

___ needs partial refinishing or touchup

___ needs complete refinishing; est. time or cost ___

___ not practical to refinish

*The different finishes are discussed in chapter 7, "Refinishing Considerations."

6

Repair and Usage Considerations

Repairs in General

Most people's first concern in choosing an item of old furniture is probably *appearance*. Considerations of style, wood, color, and finish come first because they deal with things that are visible. Practical concerns, like whether a pie safe will fit between two doorframes in the kitchen or whether a table will seat eight comfortably, usually come after the visual matters have been settled. Thoughts about damage and the need for repairs, if they surface, usually have to do with obvious defects while just as important, but more subtle ones, go unnoticed.

Most old furniture, even that which is refinished, needs some degree of repair work. To locate specific problems and to help decide whether a piece is worth buying, you need to examine it thoroughly.

With a careful and trained eye, some will prove feasible and not bring a troublesome shock once they are placed into use. Others you will see as impractical or impossible to fix and an even worse predicament will be prevented.

Many repairs are fairly easy once they have been explained clearly. Understanding a few basic procedures like gluing and clamping or the better use of screws can go a long way in accomplishing a great variety of repairs. While some repairs require the use of a good refinishing and repair book as a reference source, many of them will be understandable from what follows in this chapter.

Examining for Repairs

Examining for repairs, in general, is not difficult. In beginning an examination the first aspects to gather your attention will probably be those of general condition. Unless overshadowed by severe damage, the surface condition of the wood and its finish will stand out most. (These will be covered in the next chapter.) Once you have assessed them, look for anything needing repair. Somewhere you may want to distinguish between wear and *damage*. Unless it's excessive, wear is generally considered appropriate and is part of the age and character of a piece. Damage, on the other hand, is breakage, looseness of joints, or other more drastic conditions.

After locating damage the next step is to decide whether the piece is worth fixing and how to do it. More specific questions might include:

- Can it be fixed satisfactorily?
- What will be the total cost of the piece, including repairs? Is it worth it?
- Can you do the work yourself?
- Do you have the workspace?
- Are the necessary repair materials available?
- Do you have the needed patience? How long will it take?
- Can you find a good repairman? How much will he charge?

Poor Candidates

Sometimes the first question facing you once you have located damage is whether it can be repaired at all, or at least without getting into exorbitant costs. Some types of damage that cannot usually be repaired are:

- crushed or otherwise severely damaged carvings;
- broken lacework with parts missing;

- extensive inlay or marquetry work that is badly damaged;
- deeply weathered wood;
- burns over large areas;
- missing parts that were manufactured using special tools or processes.

Many pieces that can be repaired require such extensive work that they deserve to be ruled out. Usually the repairs are too demanding and the results to be gained are poor. Often a piece of comparable design or function can be bought for significantly less than a shabby one would cost in the long run.

Sometimes a piece that needs considerable work can only be repaired with many new wood replacement parts or other mending that is highly visible. On a piece that has many new parts, an inability to match the original wood's color and grain patterns can give it a motley appearance.

Usually just the cost or time involved in very extensive repairs makes them prohibitive. Doing the work yourself can relieve the expense, but when repairs reach sizeable proportions, the effort can become what some refinishers fecetiously call a "labor of love." Large items like pianos, Hoosier cabinets, and pump organs can easily fall into this category if they are in poor shape.

The Silk Purse

Another point of view is that if you are willing to go to extremes, you sometimes *can* make a silk purse from a sow's ear. With hours of careful work, many a dilapidated old piece can be restored miraculously, giving its owner extra satisfaction when it is completed. Such a piece should be selected carefully, however, and the price paid should be based on its actual condition, not its potential.

Decisions, Decisions

Estimating the cost of repairs is difficult, even for the professional repairman. Sometimes the best you can do, without much experience, is decide whether the work is major or minor or somewhere in between. Later sections in this chapter should give you enough information to categorize many specific kinds of work and to make reasonable decisions reflecting the effort and money you want to spend.

If you do the work yourself, your expenses are for tools and materials, not labor. Many skills can be learned from books and other sources, and many repair tools can be purchased cheaply, borrowed, or even improvised. Workspace, on the other hand, may be a problem, or you may feel your time and patience are too short or you may want a better repair job than you can do yourself. For any or all these reasons you may want to have the work done by a repairman or just decide the piece is unreasonable to buy.

The Services of a Repairman

If you decide on a repairman, it might be best to have one in mind before buying a piece that requires his skills. In some areas the repairmen who are skillful are scarce and busy with customer bookings months in advance. Those with good reputations are usually high in price.

Some individuals that repair furniture list themselves under cabinet shops, cabinetmakers, furniture restoration, millwork, or furniture stripping. Almost as often you will find repair work done in less formal settings by people working out of their garages or basements. Friends who have had work done can probably fill you in on who best to contact.

Although it is nice to be a patron of the arts and offer *carte blanche* to the repairman you select, try to get an estimate and at least an agreement that he'll call you before getting into any unforeseen work. Try to involve yourself with the repairman in planning what specifically needs to be done.

* * *

The rest of this chapter will deal with examining particular categories of furniture: tables, beds, and other major kinds. It should help you examine more closely so that you can assess not only needed repairs but also some related to home use. Because considerations of repair and use often meet in an examination, the two will be discussed together.

Tables

A table should set reasonably level—level enough to be in keeping with the age of the piece and level enough for you to enjoy it. There are two kinds of levelness. One, *the warpage of individual boards* comprising a tabletop, can be judged by sighting down the length of them and looking at their ends. *Unevenness of stance*, which may affect the levelness of the top as a whole, is either due to unequal legs or something affecting their alignment.

Unless there is something obviously broken or loose, it is difficult to evaluate stance if the floor the table sets on is itself not level. In such a situation, moving the table to a flatter surface may be necessary, but check for breakage first. Check the leg joints, the skirts, and the table slides or other understructure. After checking for breakage, look for loose hardware. The hanger bolts used to secure legs to skirts are

Top view of a table having boards warped by moisture absorption from underneath.

often loose. Loose screws going up through the skirts into the top will allow small gaps that are visible between the two parts. If the screws that connect the slides to the tabletop are not tight, the table may sag in the middle.

A pull-apart leaf table should open and close with ease, and the best test is to try it out. If the one you are considering bucks and sticks, try rubbing soap or wax between the table slides after you have extended them as far as possible. If problems persist, some screws could be loose, or the slides could be improperly installed or even broken. To be properly installed, table slides must be centered precisely in both the length and width dimensions of the tabletop. If replacement is needed, new wooden slides are available through mail order. See "General Suppliers" in chapter 9.

Replacing old table leaves or adding new ones poses problems. When hand constructed, table leaves required precise alignment, and getting them right with just hand tools was some accomplishment; making them completely interchangeable was almost impossible. Factory-made leaves became interchangeable only because of spe-

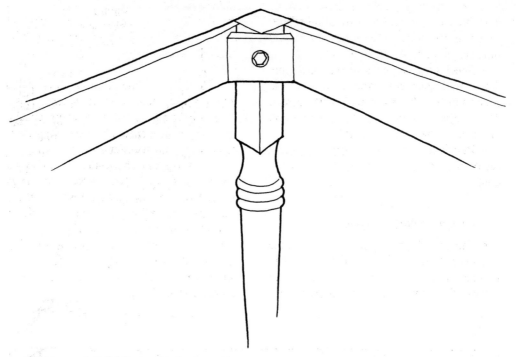

The hanger bolt holding a table leg in position is often loose and can do wonders when tightened.

cial procedures to minimize warpage and special tools for the alignment and drilling of the dowel pin holes.

If you are evaluating a table that has one or more leaves missing, open it to its maximum extension to measure its capacity. You probably can get one or two close-fitting leaves made for a moderate cost. Several leaves will involve an increasing complexity of fit and are sure to be expensive while probably not interchangeable.

Extra leaves need adequate support. A leaf table with four regular legs must have a fifth and sometimes a sixth leg if it is to be free of sag in its middle. The top halves of a pedestal leaf table also need to be well supported underneath to accommodate extra leaves.

When shopping for a drop-leaf table be sure to check for adequate seating room between the legs of the table's narrower ends. Most do not provide enough room for seating. Another thing is that many drop-leaf tables are made so that the leaves, when they are hanging, are very close to the table's legs. If you are considering removing the warpage from the top of such a table by sawing the individual boards and then edge-planing them, the saw and joiner cuts you make may narrow the top to such an extent that the leaves have to jut out.

Simple Table Repairs

• Loose screws attaching the slides or skirts to the tabletop can usually be replaced by *thicker* ones. Longer screws will probably go through the top.

• Legs that are uneven can often be equalized by the addition of dome glides to the shorter feet. Other glides, even small bottlecaps, can be used instead.

• Special leg height adjusters, available from mailorder companies, fit into the sockets of legs that were made with casters. These adjusters can be used to equalize legs or to raise their overall height.

• Paraffin wax or soap applied to any set of moving parts may make them usable.

More Difficult Table Repairs

• Table slides to replace broken ones are not too difficult to install but require a drill and countersink, a carpenter's square, and screws of the correct length. Installing new slides is a matter of centering them perpendicular to the table opening, then drilling and countersinking new screw holes with enough precision to avoid going through the top.

• Realigning slides that are off center involves the same procedures. An effort should be made, however, to avoid ending up in some of the old screw holes that caused the problem in the first place.

• New table legs are usually cut on a joiner and/or turned on a lathe. If you have any made, specify that you want one-piece stock rather than the kind that is made of several glued-together pieces.

• It is difficult to do a radical sanding job on a tabletop without revealing the screws that come up from under the table. Light sanding is usually possible, though.

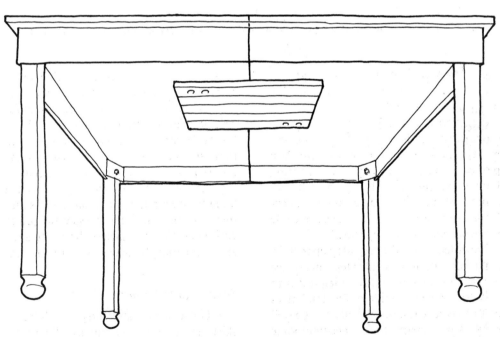

A view of a table's slide unit seen by turning the table over. The boards with the screwholes are stationary while the others move.

If a tabletop's warped boards are reduced too much, they become narrower and the table's drop-leaves may jut out.

Chairs

Chair fit is crucial for comfort. In shopping for a personal chair, be sure to try it out. To test for comfort, see if the chair's design fits your design. Seat height is most important, particularly in chairs used for eating or work. A chair that is too high or too low will disturb blood circulation and cause fatigue from muscle tension.

In an appropriately comfortable table or desk chair, you are positioned so that your back is straight or slightly reclined. Your feet are flat and your legs are nearly vertical. The backs of lounging chairs are more reclined, and their seat heights are generally lower, so that your legs stretch out. Chairs that are too low may be hard to get in and out of. If you are shopping for a set of chairs that will be average enough to suit people of various heights, choose seat heights between 18 and 19½ inches.

Slant-back chairs for table use are often

The use of dome glides such as this one is a good way to even-up furniture legs.

more comfortable than the straight ones associated with formal dining. Chairs with padded seats also offer comfort, particularly while sitting for long periods.

In terms of construction, a chair has got to be tough. Not only does it bear more weight, proportionately, than almost any other furniture, but the weight shifts and leans. Because of this, a chair should have strong parts that are tightly joined. It should also have an all-points stance to prevent uneven stress on its joints. The back and arms, if it has arms, must be well suppported, and the legs should have at least one stretcher (rung) between them. Rockers need more.

Some of the joints that are most important are the leg-to-bottom joints under the seat. For stability of the lower chair parts, the leg ends should fit snugly and deeply into the seat. To test them, wrap your hand firmly around the top of each leg and pry up against the bottom of the chair. If the joints are simply loose, they can be considered basically sound and the repairs not too complicated. Wobbly joints, on the other hand, are fairly indicative of poor construction, breakage, or poor prior repairs.

What applies to loose leg-to-bottom joints applies to most of the others. While some broken spindles and rungs can be

repaired with little or no dismantling, others require that whole sections be taken apart. Broken parts that are reasonably intact can often be mended, but when breaks are beyond repair, new parts must be made, then finished and assembled back into the chair.

An empty rocking chair should set only moderately backwards. If the back is too far reclined, it's usually due to wear on the rockers. Wear that is not too far advanced can sometimes be compensated by using weights under the front of the seat. If replacement rockers are needed, they must be made enough like the original so that the chair will have its proper stance. The new rockers must be carefully drilled before installation so that the chair legs fit into them very well.

If you are considering buying a chair that needs a new caned or woven seat, check with the people in your area for an estimate. Costs can run very high. There are two varieties of caning to consider. Machine-woven cane is the kind held in place by gluing a long wedge into a groove that

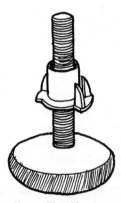

A leg height adjuster like this one may be helpful to raise the height of something originally having casters. You may decide you prefer casters to its metal and Bakelite appearance.

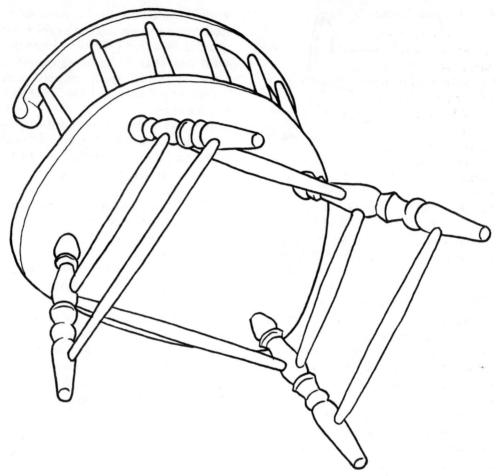

A chair's leg ends, for stability, must fit tightly into the chair's bottom. Placing a very heavy weight on the seat of the chair once you are done gluing is one of the best methods. Sitting and wiggling around on the seat helps the legs fit tightly before the weight is used.

surrounds the cut-out portion of a chair. Handwoven cane, which costs considerably more, is laced through a system of holes drilled into the perimeter of the cut-out portion.

Country chairs often have seats woven from any of a variety of materials. The usual replacement materials include seagrass, Kraft paper rush (originally rush was made from cattail leaves), and ash or oak splints. A professional shop will have an assortment of materials. In considering a cane bottom chair that has an embossed fiber replacement seat, don't assume that the wood underneath it is in good condition. Damage from tacks used to hold prior replacements is very common and sometimes difficult to repair well.

Simple Chair Repairs

• A solid chair seat that is split can be rejoined with glue and long clamps but dirt, paint, and other substances must first be cleaned out. Careful removal is needed to keep the crack's edges intact.

• When joints are only slightly loose, the use of a wood swelling agent called *Chair-loc* can often make them tight again.

• For chair legs that are uneven, the addition of small domed glides to the shorter legs is preferred to cutting off the longer ones and ending up with a shorter chair.

• A chair that is too low can usually benefit from a seat cushion.

More Difficult Chair Repairs

• Regluing loose chair joints is often complicated because of a domino effect that occurs when one joint is weakened. Frequently it is necessary to dismantle and reglue adjacent joints in addition to the ones that obviously need attention.

• Reassembling a dismantled chair requires correct labeling of parts beforehand. Sometimes parts must be rejoined in a certain sequence. Reassembly requires correct alignment, and all the parts of a major section usually must be completed together. The legs and their stretchers, for instance, must be joined together *and* the leg ends inserted into the seat, all in one step. Unless you have a sure reassembly plan beforehand, you should use a slow-drying glue. In either case, a heavy weight must be used to "clamp" the inserted leg ends.

Furniture with Drawers

Drawer dovetailing is likely the first construction feature a dealer will display to impress you. Although helpful, it is no guarantee of sturdiness. The working condition, fit, and materials are other signs of drawer workmanship to consider.

A reliable drawer must fit in several dimensions. A good fit front to back depends on its *drawer stops*, usually small blocks of wood glued to the top or bottom of the inside of the drawer frame. The stops keep the front of the drawer in line with the

A split in a chair's bottom needs to be cleaned out carefully before gluing and clamping.

frame. The working parts, the *runners* and *drawer slides*, function to maintain the up-and-down positioning of the drawer and provide for moving the drawer in and out. The *runners*, in the great majority of old furniture, are the lower side edges of the drawer itself. The *slides* on which the runners travel are built into the inside of the cabinet. Usually there is a *side stop* nailed and glued to each of the slides to provide the sideways fit of the drawer.

Factory-built drawers were, in general, cheaply made. While their fronts were made of the same material and thickness as the surrounding cabinet, the bottoms, backs, and sides, which needed to be almost as stout, were mostly made of thin pieces of pine and poplar too soft for long wear. Factory drawer bottoms were usually held in place with nails. Because the wood was soft and thin and tended to warp and flex with weight, the nails have often worked loose over the years. The working drawer parts, the runner and the slides, also made of soft woods, soon wore down after continual opening and closing.

Handmade cabinets, while they vary in quality, were generally made with thicker parts that provide more rigidity. Often their drawer slides were made of denser, longer-wearing woods, which hold up better against opening and closing. Very close grained pine, much thicker and harder than the usual, was a frequent choice.

The best handmade drawers often had *raised panel bottoms* and were dovetailed front *and* back. Both features provided more strength and freedom from warpage.

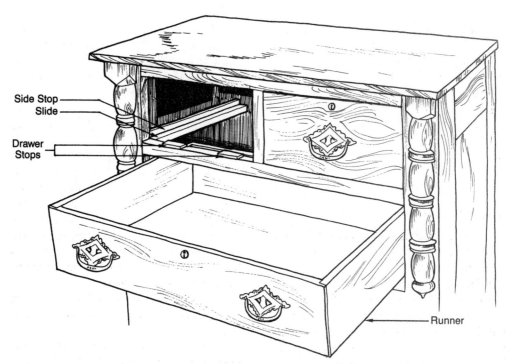

Side Stop

Slide

Drawer Stops

Runner

A view of a chest of drawers showing its working parts.

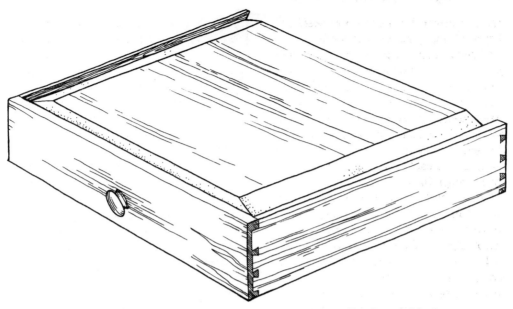

A handmade drawer showing its panelled bottom and dovetailing front and back.

Dovetailing, incidently, is a joining method primarily used to prevent warpage and loosening of the drawer front and sides by providing an interlocking grip between them. By itself it does not guarantee good construction. For durability a drawer must also fit tightly enough within its stops to prevent it from joggling around when it's opened and closed.

Simple Drawer Repairs

• A good half measure to use with worn runners and slides is to fill just the slides with epoxy putty.

• Drawer bottoms that are damaged can sometimes be replaced with plywood, masonite, or wall paneling. The use of glued-together boards planed to the correct thickness is the preferred method but is, of course, much more expensive.

• New nails or screws will sometimes tighten loose parts, but don't use nails in the same old holes. To prevent splitting, don't nail too close to board ends or edges. (Nails, while they are frowned on by connoisseurs, may be necessary or sufficient in a given situation. They were used often by the original craftsmen.)

• Stuck drawers will often work well enough when soap or wax is applied to their runners or slides or around drawer front edges. If sanding the edges of a drawer front becomes necessary, be conservative and sand only a little at a time to prevent visible gaps between the drawer front and the cabinet frame. Be careful not to round off the edges or corners.

• New drawer stops can be made from small blocks of wood glued and clamped into place.

• Thumb tacks can be inserted in the front of slides that are only slightly worn.

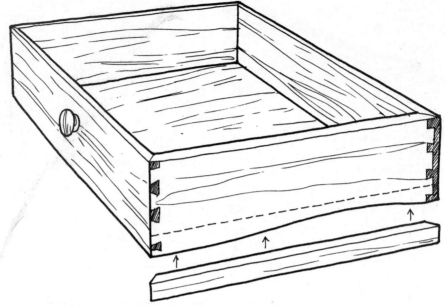

A drawer runner to be sawn off and replaced. Replacing the lower dovetailing is more than twice as expensive.

More Difficult Drawer Repairs

• When a drawer runner is worn badly, the usual and most practical solution involves the use of a table saw to remove the worn section of the drawer side (the runner) a fraction above the damage. A new strip of harder wood is then glued and clamped in place of the sawed-off section.

• Exacting repairs that involve the reworking of dovetailing will require special skills and will probably be expensive. In many cases of repairing worn runners, however, the lowest dovetail may be sacrificed when adding a new strip to a drawer side.

• New slides with slide stops attached are easy to make but may be hard to install. In many cases several can be made at one time by gluing several feet of side stop material to an equal length of stock suitable for slides. Individual units are then made by subdividing the longer lengths. Some additional small cuts may be necessary to install slides within the cabinet. The difficulty in installing the units usually lies in having precise enough measurements and in making the slides fit level and tight within the cabinet's interior framework.

Furniture with Doors

Old furniture doors, as found on sideboards, pie safes, and many other items were constructed in the following basic ways:

• from one or more solid boards, sometimes with raised centers;
• as panels with plain or raised centers;
• as panels with centers made of plywood, glass, or tin;
• with veneer, especially on curved doors.

Door construction required considerable skill. In order for doors to fit and open and close easily, both they and their surrounding frames had to be square, flat, precisely measured, and properly installed. Although considerable pain had to be taken in construction and installation, there could not be an absolute guarantee that they would stay in alignment under conditions of hard use and humidity change.

Many doors do present problems. Through continued use or because they were not of sufficient quality, many of their hinges have become bent, loose, or broken. Sometimes they have been forced out of position by warpage of the door parts caused by humidity acting on twisted grain patterns within the wood. Many times also there has been a simple swelling of parts by excessive humidity. In other instances gaps between door parts have developed when wood that had not dried sufficiently was used in construction.

The latches and catches on many old cabinets were an integral part of door construction. They helped achieve alignment and kept doors from coming open by themselves. In country furniture the simplest was a *block* and *screw latch* used to hold one door in line with another. The other usually

Four types of door construction.

was anchored by an *eyelet catch* holding it to a shelf inside the cabinet. (See "Hardware" in chapter 9.)

Finer furniture often employed *cupboard turn knobs* that could be rotated to open and closed positions. (See chapter 9 for knobs also.) Factory doors were frequently made secure with stops, small blocks of wood similar to those used with drawers. To hold doors closed, key locks were often used in conjunction with stops or by themselves. In the late 1800s more sophisticated latches and catches were invented for factory furniture. Many of them made use of internal springs that made opening and closing more automatic.

Simple Door Repairs

• With a poorly fitting door, check the hinges first. Sometimes they only need to be straightened by squeezing in a vise or pounding them flat with a hammer.

• Missing or bent hinge pins can often be replaced with a roundhead nail.

• When hinge screw holes have become enlarged, *longer* screws can be inserted in place of the old ones. Be careful that the new screws are not so thick that they split the wood.

• Shims made of small thicknesses of wood or paper placed behind hinges can often compensate for poor alignment.

• Doors that stick can be sanded or planed for a better fit, but check hinges first.

• Moving an existing latch or adding a new one can sometimes bring doors into alignment with their frames and with each other.

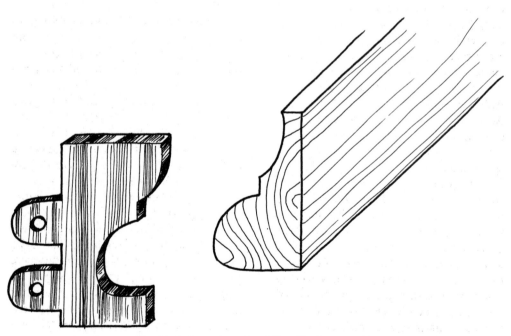

A new cutting blade for a piece of molding. Fits into a molding machine.

More Difficult Door Repairs

• Broken or badly warped door parts may need replacement. Power tools are needed and repairman costs are usually high. Molded contouring on any of the parts may require making new cutting blades for use with a molding machine, but their cost is usually low compared with labor and materials.

• Reassembling dismantled door parts requires the use of a square, bar or pipe clamps, and precise alignment.

• Mild to moderate warpage may require repositioning hinges, sanding or planing door edges, and the movement or addition of appropriate latches and catches.

Beds

Don't buy an old bed unless you are *completely* sure you can find a mattress that will fit both it and your pocketbook. Old hand-made beds and the straw or feather tickings used with them were made with the often eccentric reckonings of the craftsmen who made them or according to the desires or dimensions of their individual customers. Although factory-made beds achieved standard widths in the late 1800s, their lengths still varied until the 1920s or so.

In order to provide enough room for sheets and covers, a mattress should ideally be 3 to 5 inches less in length than the bedframe used with it. To provide a snug fit that prevents shifting within its bedframe, it should be close to the same width as the inside distance between the side rails. While a mattress that is wider or narrower can be used, too much deviation will affect appearance or comfortable use of the bed.

If you buy an old bed that needs a custom-made mattress, locating a company to make it may be a problem. If you do locate a mattress shop, you are likely to find that the quality you're used to is high priced — a custom shop cannot compete with factory production methods. You may have to pay the same for blue striped ticking in a custom mattress that you would for floral quilted quality in one that is factory-made.

Some old beds are shorter than even people of average height can tolerate. The usual solutions are to replace side rails entirely or to lengthen them by splicing on an additional section. Either proposition is likely to be expensive. Bed length may not be the only problem, however. Many old beds were built with a very high mattress height. Some even required a footstool for getting in and out. In many cases such a situation can be compensated by lowering the slat support strips attached to the side rails. If moving them is insufficient, L-shaped brackets of heavy steel can be installed to hold the mattress in a still lower position.

Many *metal* beds have beautiful curves and turnings that make them tempting, but like wooden beds, they come with the same problem — that of trying to find a suitable mattress. Although you may find a bed that seems to accommodate a modern mattress size, don't buy it without making *exact* measurements and allowances. If you can solve the problem of mattress fit and decide on buying a particular metal bed, be sure to get the right side rails. Although several rail ends may look similar, they are seldom interchangeable.

Getting rid of rust is the main problem in repainting steel or iron beds. One of the best ways to remove it is with a rotary wire brush used with an electric drill. Figure on eight hours or more for thorough removal of very bad rust, the heavy orange scale that develops when bare metal has been left outdoors a season or more. Even a rust accu-

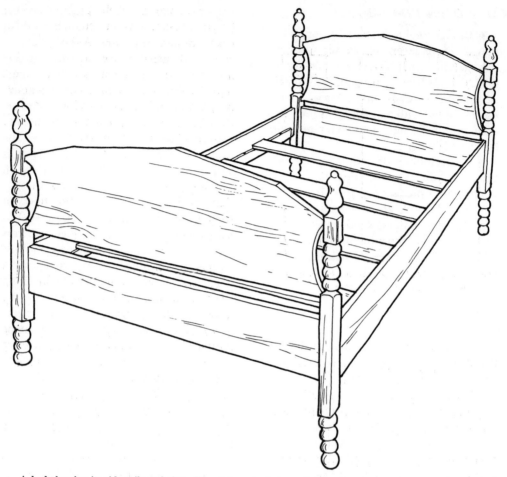

A bed showing its side rails and slats. The slat supports can often be moved to provide more comfort.

mulation of a few days will take at least two hours. (These figures are based on almost total rust removal, which is usually necessary to prevent any of it from eventually coming through a new paint job.) If you are planning to get a metal bed dip-stripped, ask that it be wiped down to dry off the rinse water used after it comes out of the stripping tank. This will eliminate much of the type of rust that accumulates quickly after the immersion.

Furniture with Shelves

Among the things that contain shelves are bookcases, secretaries, china cabinets, and hutches. Although aesthetically they range from the purely functional to the highly decorative, they all need to be evaluated in practical terms before buying. Shelves by themselves are usually simple devices. What mainly differentiates them are their size and whether they are fas-

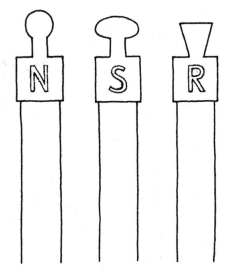

Metal bed rail ends. There were about fifteen different patterns, each lettered separately.

Determining the shelf space needed for books is best done by measuring and dividing them into categories. Although bookcases with tiered shelves accommodating different sizes are sometimes available, most only have a single *depth*. For a general-purpose bookcase, the depth should be at least 9½ inches. If you are measuring the various sizes of your books, you may have categories that resemble these in *height*:

Category	Height
Paperbacks	7½" to 8"
Medium books	9¼" to 10"
Large books	12¼" to 13¼"

Records are larger than most books and may need special consideration if you plan to shelve them. A shelf that is enclosed with glass doors must have a height of twelve and a half inches and even more depth to allow the doors to close. If the shelf has no doors, it can, of course, be shorter in depth, leaving the albums protruding a little. One

tened or adjustable. Adjustable shelves have the obvious advantage of accommodating objects of various heights.

Some of the important questions in determining the suitability of shelves are as follows:

- How much linear shelf space is needed?
- How deep and how high must the shelves be?
- How much deviation from an ideal fit can be tolerated?
- How much room is needed for growth?
- Is extra strength needed to hold especially heavy objects, such as a set of encyclopedias?
- What specific requirements must be met to display a collection, art objects, or artifacts?
- Are glass-enclosed shelves needed to reduce aging and dust accumulation of valuable possessions?

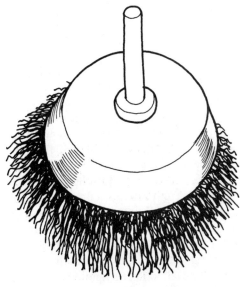

A rotary wire brush of a versatile type.

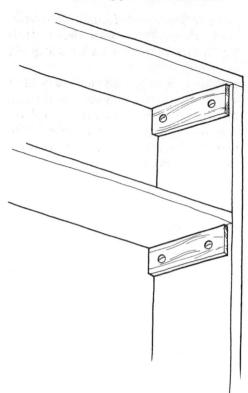

Shelves with simple support brackets. Moving the brackets is easy unless they have been glued.

linear foot of shelf space will maximally hold about seventy single albums.

Other things that you may want to store on shelves may need careful measurement and planning. Most stereo components, because of their depth, will not fit most bookshelves. Many magazines present problems because they don't have the rigidity to stand up unsupported. Annual container boxes, the kind found in libraries, seem to be the best solution for them.

Ideally, the taller a bookcase, the greater its stance should be to prevent its falling over. The likelihood of a tipover is increased on deeply carpeted floors and with chil-

dren. Placing heavier items on lower shelves or fastening the framework to the wall may be the only solutions for a bookcase that is satisfactory otherwise.

Simple Shelf Repairs

• Shelves that are not level or stable can often be compensated by using small paper or wooden shims between them and their supports.

• Even though most bookcases do not make allowances for depth differences, you can make paperbacks and other small books stay at the front edges of their shelves by putting boxes or other spacers behind them.

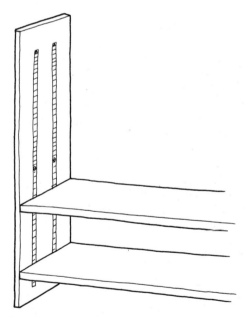

A modern pair of adjuster strips for bookshelves. Old furniture shelves were often made adjustable in other clever ways.

More Difficult Shelf Repairs

• Shelves that are positioned undesirably can usually be moved. The job is easy for shelves that are held in place by simple support brackets underneath them. The job is harder, and may require some refinishing touchup, if the shelves are nailed into place from the outside of the cabinet. If nails have been sunk with a nail punch, it is best to try to saw them off from inside. A hacksaw blade will usually work. Tape its leading surface to prevent its scratching the wood.

• Both the nailed and unnailed types of shelves can usually be made variable with the installation of adjuster strips, available at many hardware stores. Most shelves need to be shortened slightly to make room for the strips, however.

7

Refinishing Considerations

Refinishing

This chapter is partly a shopper's guide to refinishing and partly an introduction to refinishing in general. It should help you be more selective about buying furniture and provide a worthwhile set of viewpoints on refinishing materials and procedures. Even if you decide not to do the refinishing yourself, it should give you a good idea of what refinishers themselves do and a better basis for communicating the things you want done. A few things that will be said in the chapter relate directly to buying already finished furniture, but the bulk of the discussion about it is back in chapter 5, "Examining Old Furniture."

What It Is

The process of refinishing is essentially one of taking off an old finish and putting on a new one. A finish itself has two basic functions: to protect the wood and to beautify it. The most prevalent kinds of finish used on old furniture were shellac and paint.

More Than One Would Suppose

Much antique furniture for sale, particularly at flea markets and auctions, does need attention. The work required, beginning with removing the old finish, can vary a great deal. Sometimes with furniture that needs refinishing you are in a position to save considerably compared with furniture that is already redone. Frequently, however, and especially on items that are in poor condition, you can get caught with far more work and expense than you ever imagined. Similarly designed pieces can vary 300 percent or more in the time it takes to do them. Usually the differences are in stripping, surface repairs, and sanding. The 300 percent figure is just for refinishing. If repairs are needed, the differences can be much higher. As related earlier, about a quarter of the old furniture on today's market falls in a 300 percent category.

Getting a Rough Idea

When deciding whether to buy a piece, you must have more than intuition about the work it needs. If you're to do the work yourself, you need at least a basic idea of the time involved, or to be able to translate it into labor costs if you're going to hire a refinisher.

In some sense it is only fair that the worth of a finished piece at least be equal to the work that goes into it. There's a lot to be said, however, about the rewards of long, hard work that turns a dilapidated old piece into something restored to a charming and useful condition. The common denominator of both viewpoints is that there must be a worthwhile finished product.

Although a great variation in refinishing times is to be expected, given all the various problems that add difficulty, the majority of pieces that have only their original finish and no more than one coat of paint or other finish added can be considered in an average category of refinishing ease. Here is a list of times for several kinds of "average" furniture. Repair times are not included.

5–10 hours — chairs, small tables, small hall stands

10–20 hours — chests of drawers, large tables, small desks, beds

20–40 hours — medium desks, sideboards, corner cupboards

40–80 hours — roll-top desks, secretary desks, pianos

As you can see in the list, the more complex, larger pieces not only take more time, but also are more variable. They are also less predictable. As stated, the chart is just for pieces with an average level of difficulty. Add more coats of finish or other conditions of complexity, and the lengths of time will increase.

The rest of the chapter will consist of general information about refinishing. Its purpose is to give you perspective on each of the steps in a normal refinishing sequence, but it will not deal much with the details of how to do refinishing itself. The details here are the basic ones that you should know while shopping and examining. A great deal will concern stripping in its several aspects.

Refinishing Steps in Sequence

The normal steps in a refinishing sequence are as follows:

- stripping*
- surface preparation
- staining
- finish coats
- rubbing down

Stripping

Before Stripping

Stripping is the process of removing an old finish to make way for a new one, but

---

*General repairs usually come before or just after stripping.

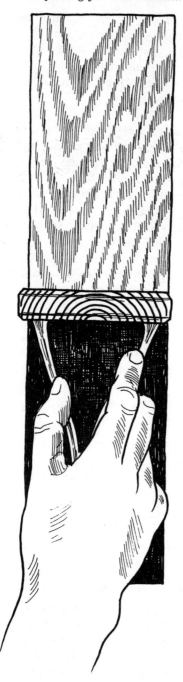

Fake graining produced by the use of ink over paint and manipulated by a graining tool.

it should not be done automatically with every piece of furniture. Some finishes, even the ordinary, are worth saving and just need to be cleaned (usually done with Varsol or some other paint thinner) to remove grain-imbedded particles and surface dust. It is particularly desirable to preserve the following finishes unless they are in poor condition:

- milk paint, blood paint;
- Pennsylvania Dutch decoration; decorative painting on any country furniture, stenciling on fancy chairs and Boston rockers;
- fake graining, marbleizing and swirling, sponge painting;
- Oriental lacquering, Eastlake paint;
- cottage furniture decoration and paint.

Milk paint used milk as a vehicle and pigments bought from the general store or from peddlers. Blood paint was grisly. It used dark pigments and the blood that was available at slaughter time.

Fake graining, marbleizing, etc. were all decorative effects created with paint and such tools as sponges, feathers, and quills. Fake graining began as a homecraft skill but became more sophisticated when taken over by the factories around the turn of the century. At about the same time commercially produced tools for fake graining became available to the home handyman and the painting trade.

Of the various species of wood, oak was the one imitated by graining tools most often. In the early 1900s it was imitated on poplar using factory stenciling techniques. Plainer pieces of furniture that look like oak are the ones to check to see if the wood grain is real or imitation. The grain in fake graining has less definition.

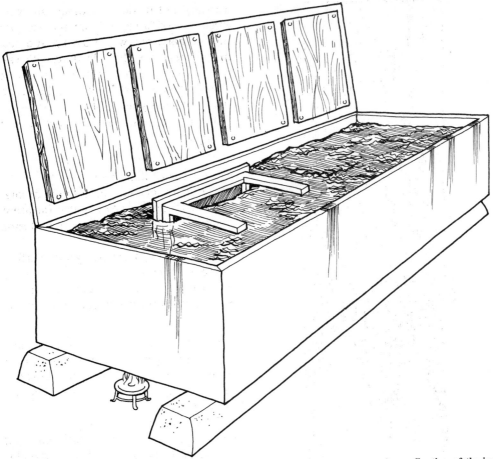

A heated tank containing alkalis dissolved in water. The boards on the lid are to curb any floating of the immersed furniture.

Hand-Stripping vs. Dip-stripping

If an item you are considering clearly needs stripping, the first question you'll probably ask is whether to strip it yourself or get it dip-stripped. Doing it yourself, you know, involves plenty of work, but you've heard dip-stripping can lead to problems. Although strong opinions can be found, there is no simple answer to which method is best. Each has its advantages in meeting different stripping circumstances. To help you make decisions about which method to use, the discussions that follow compare the two.

Hand-Stripping Applications

The kind of hand-stripping to be discussed is one that uses commercial paint and varnish removers that are usually cleaned up with alcohol or Varsol and are available at most hardware stores. There are removers that require water for cleanup, but since they offer no overall advantages, they will not be considered. The others are by far the widest in use. The kind of dip-stripping to be compared in this section employs a heated tank containing alkalis dissolved in water. It is the widest immersion process in use.

Hand-stripping has two broad advantages, particularly if you do the work yourself. One is the care it affords fine, delicate furniture and dark-colored woods. A safe handling of pieces with fragile joints is more certain, and walnut, mahogany, and other dark woods keep their true colors better.

Hand-stripping is needed for objects with marquetry or inlay work and is the safest method for ordinary veneer. It is also the best for furniture having several coats of paint. While dip-stripping can remove many paint layers, it almost always requires a prolonged soaking time. The greater water absorption tends to bring out warpage, cracking, and raised grain. While hand-stripping does mean harder work, it avoids these problems.

Dip-stripping Applications

Among the several advantages of dip-stripping, the one most people look to is its work savings — dip-stripping does save work in most cases. With most pieces it also does a good job with minimal risk.

Unfortunately the conditions under which dip-stripping operates best are the ones that are the easiest for hand-stripping also. Pieces with their original finish or those with few additional coats are stripped quickly without much disturbance to the wood. Other furniture may be different. Pieces with many coats of paint are subject to all the problems of water absorption mentioned earlier, plus they are usu-

ally left with a significant amount of the paint in cracks, grooves, and joints. Strippers usually have to leave this work for the owner or charge extra, sometimes a lot extra.

Dip-stripping should not be dismissed as inferior overall because of the problems it presents with many coats of finish. It can do a good job on pieces having just a few layers and can accomplish some jobs that are impossible by hand methods. Because of its immersion process, dip-stripping can strip wicker furniture completely. It can also, unlike hand-stripping, "pull" many types of paint and woodstain that has penetrated pores. Hand-stripping sometimes only increases their absorption into the wood.

A by-product of dip-stripping is that it sanitizes and deodorizes a piece on all its surfaces, not just the convenient exterior parts. It also kills any boring insects that may have gotten into the wood.

A disadvantage of dip-stripping is that it requires that a piece be left to dry for several days after coming out of the tank. Dip-stripped pieces also require a degree of sanding to smooth raised grain. How much sanding will be discussed later on.

The Hand-Stripping Process

As you can see from the discussion, neither hand-stripping nor dip-stripping can be considered the better method for all conditions. Each one, rather, is suited for a particular set of circumstances, and most jobs can be done equally well by either. Deciding which to use in those circumstances when it doesn't matter gets into questions of economics, time, energy, and your local dip-stripper's reputation. To help you decide further, here is a sequence of the basic steps in hand-stripping:

Step 1. *Cleaning a piece to remove dirt.* This is only necessary if there is a lot of dirt and is done to prevent it from getting into the wood. Soot, or anything like it, must absolutely be cleaned away before stripping. If the old finish is intact, mineral spirits (Varsol) or turpentine is used with a rag. If places of bare wood exist and dirt has gotten into them, dip-stripping is preferred because of its "floating" action. In general, furniture with imbedded dirt is a bad buy. Some of the dirt is likely to remain in the wood.

Step 2. *Applying paint and varnish remover.* The best type consists of methyline chloride, one or two other ingredients, but no *toluol* or *acetone* (these are contained only in the cheaper, less effective products). To begin stripping, the remover is usually flowed on in a heavy coat with a brush and allowed to work a very minimum of 10 minutes. Several coats of paint may require several coats of remover and up to an hour's wait. Enough remover and enough patience are the keys to an effective job with the least wasted effort.

Step 3. *Removing the gunk.* This is first done with a paint scraper to remove the bulk of it and then with steel wool to remove the rest. To do a complete job of cleaning up, denatured alcohol or mineral spirits is needed with most brands of remover. One of the two is used carefully with steel wool followed with a dry rag or paper towel. More than one cleanup may be needed.

Dip-Stripping Basics

There are essentially two kinds of dip-stripping, but the one using a *hot tank* is by far the widest in use. The other method, the *cold tank*, does a better job in some respects but is not available in most areas and is more expensive, often much more. A lower-priced variation of the cold tank process uses the same chemicals but applies them with a flow-on method. The very latest stripping process, about which little information is available, does the work of removing old finishes using vapors released in sealed chambers. Because the hot tank methods are the most prevalent, the information that follows will center on them.

The chemicals contained in the hot tank are alkalis dissolved in water. To intensify their action, the solution is heated to a temperature of about 150 degrees Fahrenheit. Both temperature and pH must be kept at a near constant level. The alkali solution is mild enough that many stripping operators wash their hands with it and receive no harmful effects.

In the hot tank system a furniture item is totally submerged. How long it remains varies greatly and depends on the kind of old finish and how thick it is. Frequently an easy piece will only take 30 minutes, while a very difficult one may have to be dipped again and again or left for a number of hours.

Following an appropriate amount of immersion, a water rinse is employed to remove finish residues that have not fallen off or gone into solution. After a water rinse, a weak oxalic acid solution is sprayed on to retard the wood's darkening from exposure to the water.

There are several critical areas in dip-stripping that determine the quality of a job and the possibility of damage to the wood. The most important of them are:

Water immersion time. Despite all that's been said about the possibility of water damage in the hot tank, it usually only occurs with pieces that are submerged for a very long time. Pieces having a number of coats of paint are the most susceptible.

Loading-Unloading. Old furniture is often not as respected as it needs to be. One reason is that it is painstaking to handle it carefully day after day. Better dip-strippers, like anyone who moves furniture for a living, adapt themselves to the need, however.

Drying rate. Drying must be even and slow and use no heat. Circulated air works best. Because of the water immersion, drying is more critical with the hot tank process. After rinsing, any water that is standing on top surfaces must be removed to prevent warpage. Although wiping with rags is needed in many cases, most stripping shops simply tilt furniture against a wall to speed runoff. To prevent warpage, some types of furniture construction need to be clamped or weighted down during drying.

Stretching the chemicals. This is a temptation that confronts the stripper employing the hot tank. Chemicals cost money and he has to make them last as long as they can continue to strip effectively. If he uses them too long, or replaces his spillover with plain water rather than an amount of chemicals equal to the amount lost, his process is going to take longer and involve more immersion time.

Joint seal. Many people have an exaggerated notion that dip-stripping causes

Tilting furniture against a wall to speed runoff. Only circulating air (not heat) may be used for further drying.

joints to come apart by softening the glue. The truth is, that while it does happen occasionally, the loosening of joints happens far more often for another reason: broken glue seals. With a sound wood joint, the glue is intact and shields the joint's internal wood from water. A joint that has its glue seal broken has some degree of looseness that, however slight, allows water to enter and swell the inside. The swelling further loosens the joint.

Often a conflict with the stripper results when joints with broken seals were only assumed to be tight before stripping. Such joints, including those that were noticeably loose, may even appear sound after stripping, but will later loosen when the water that has gotten inside finally dries and the wood shrinks. Ideally, furniture with loose joints should be glued before being taken for dip-stripping.

Special Problems in Stripping

Except where noted, the problems discussed below are found in both hand-stripping and dip-stripping. Taking them into account when shopping can save a lot of frustration later on.

Several coats of paint over bare wood. One or two coats of paint over an original finish are ordinarily easy to remove, but when there is bare wood directly under it, the paint has more texture to cling to. Wood that has large, open pores makes for extra difficulty. An amateur paint job, the kind most frequently encountered, generally presents more problems because the paint was usually brushed into cracks, grooves, and crevices.

Dirty bare wood. Furniture that has been kept on porches, in outbuildings, and in cellars frequently has accumulated dirt and become bare of some of its finish. The dirt

has often gone deeply into the wood and generally cannot be removed well in a stripping process. It usually must be sanded away, obscured with dark stain, or left as is. Several other problems, including mildew and dry rot, are often found on such pieces.

Red mahogany stain in the wood. The dark red stain found on many furniture pieces cannot be completely removed despite what some strippers advertise about removing stains in general. Some of it almost always remains in the wood and needs to be covered by restaining.

Milk paint. With hand-stripping the removing of milk paint is a tearful process involving the use of household ammonia. With dip-stripping it is generally no problem.

Surface Preparation

Repairs normally follow stripping. Since repairs are covered in chapter 6, "Repair and Usage Considerations," the step that follows them, surface preparation, is next. There are two processes generally involved in surface preparation: repairing surface damage and smoothing the wood.

Surface Damage

As has probably been said beyond exhaustion, some surface damage, especially dents and bruises and the rubbing down of edges and corners, comes under normal wear. As long as it is not extreme, it is considered acceptable and needs no particular attention. On country furniture, especially primitives, some of it may even be desirable. The kind of surface damage that goes beyond wear is the type that needs patching or some other measure to make it less noticeable. Some of the most frequent and dramatic kinds of surface damage include:

- Black waterstains—because they frequently result from condensation on glasses and other containers, they often are shaped like black rings.
- White waterstains—these are waterstains that generally go into the finish but do not penetrate the wood. They are totally removed by stripping in the great majority of cases, but there are instances when the black stain is underneath them.
- Other stains from ink, bleach, food, perfume, lampblack, kerosene, whale oil, and many others.
- Burns from irons, candles, and cigarettes.
- Knife cuts, hatchet marks, holes from drilling.
- Mildew and dry rot.
- Termite and ant excavations.
- Mice and rat holes.
- Holes bored by worms and beetles.

In this list the only kinds of damage that can be repaired with any ease are waterstains*, mildew*, and some inks*. Even these repairs sometimes leave traces in the wood. The other stains generally cannot be removed without deep sanding.

A burn that is more than just superficial presents a difficult problem in that its char must be scraped away and replaced with a patching material. *Shellac stick*, a repair product that comes in dozens of shades and is melted into a damaged spot, is considered the ideal solution but is not easily available and requires some experience in handling. Using paint to cover superficial burns is practical in some cases.

Cuts, holes, and gouges ideally need shellac stick, but usually end up with plastic wood. Plastic wood is actually not a bad solution if you can color it properly.

Termite and ant holes usually go much deeper than what shows on the surface and may require graft-type repairs, the use of epoxy putty, or the replacement of whole parts. Mice, rat, and worm holes are usually kept for their quaintness.

Smoothing the Wood

Some kind of wood smoothing is involved in every refinishing project. As long as it does not go too deep, the wood's *patina*, its thin age layer, is preserved and will remain as one of the furniture's main aspects of beauty. Patina is the mellowness of the surface of old furniture achieved mainly by the aging of wood through oxidation. As it ages, wood generally darkens and becomes subdued. Some woods, even though they normally tend to darken, are lightened by exposure to sunlight and become more beautiful unless the light is too direct and uneven.

The aging of wood is one process. What is added to the wood, the finish, also has a patina. The finish layer, which also oxidizes, usually gets darker and may have a softened luster developed through the rubbing involved in cleaning, polishing, and waxing. Although stripping the finish and its kind of patina may destroy some of the authenticity in a piece having museum value, with most pieces a more important consideration is appearance. With today's refinishing materials, the soft luster removed in stripping most old finishes can

---

*The usual treatment for these is *oxalic acid*. Most refinishing books discuss its use. It is not always successful and can damage veneer and discolor dark woods. Use it on light-colored solid woods, oak especially.

easily be replaced and even improved. A high degree of authenticity is retained because the patina of the wood is largely left intact.

Keeping the wood's patina in good condition is the prime consideration when it comes to smoothing the wood after stripping. With hand-stripping, some smoothing is always needed to remove residues of the old finish and any of the paint and varnish remover that remains. Often, because old furniture was poorly sanded when it was constructed, it is desirable to smooth the wood to improve its feel. Frequently a dramatic difference occurs in the final results.

After hand-stripping, an improvement of the wood's texture is generally accomplished using either steel wool or sandpaper. Any of the medium grades of steel wool can be used without fear of damaging the wood's patina. The same is not true for sandpaper, however, but because most patina in old furniture is $1/16$ inch thick or more, some of the finer grades can be used in moderation.

Dip-stripping with the hot tank usually results in a need for sanding. On easy pieces that are only submerged for a few minutes, the steel wooling or sanding needed is very light. Pieces that have to remain for longer periods usually emerge with raised grain that may need considerable sanding. The sanding required can be a very sizeable job.

Someone once said that dip-stripping *heavily* painted pieces is an ironical 95 percent–5 percent proposition. You pay the stripper to remove 95 percent of the paint, but his efforts are only 5 percent of the total time involved. Removing the remaining paint and doing the sanding needed to smooth raised grain makes up the other 95 percent. It is often true, unfortunately.

Staining

This section has to do with the kind of stain used to color wood, not the stains that come from accidental spilling. First there will be some information about removing the stain that was used on old furniture and then some about the use of stain in a refinishing process.

Stripping Stained Woods

After an item of furniture has been stripped, what is left is either plain natural wood or wood that has some degree of stain still in it. The result depends on how the wood was finished originally. Woods with an attractive grain and color were usually finished with a clear shellac or varnish and will remain natural after stripping. Woods not considered as attractive were usually stained or painted.

There were *three* general processes of staining. Woods that would take color easily were simply stained and a clear finish added. Staining that was done in this way varies in its stripping ease, depending on the wood's absorption and the penetrating ability of the stain used. With some combinations of wood and stain, the stain is removed evenly but a shadow of it remains. If the shadow is dim enough, the piece can be restained or even left alone. With other combinations the stain residues are left in *patches* where the wood is more porous and the piece must be stained darkly to obscure them. Some stain, on the other hand, that was applied to bare wood is no problem to remove and comes off totally.

So far what has been discussed is stain applied to most kinds of wood. Woods like birch and maple, which do not take color well, required a deeply *penetrating* stain and were afterward coated with a finishing material that also contained stain. Because the stain applied to bare wood was extra strong, it is especially difficult to remove.

The third process of staining utilized just stain that was added to the finish. The first finish to be used with stain was shellac. Later varnish and lacquer were each combined with it. Mixing the two ingredients was a great boon to the factories. It enabled them to eliminate a step in the finishing process. If you are confronted by just a stain that was combined with finish, you will find that it is almost completely removed by either hand-stripping or dip-stripping.

If you are considering buying a piece that appears stained, a simple test of paint remover will tell you which kind of stain you will have to contend with. It can also help eliminate the ones that require far more work while at the same time yielding poorer results.

Using Stain in Refinishing

Probably the most important thing you should know about this subject is that the popular trend is to leave furniture woods natural rather than to use stain. According to today's taste, stain is used only when it is necessary to cover old stain residues that remain after stripping or to restain woods that are nondescript.

However, another outlook—one which largely ended in the sixties—was high on the use of stain. Although it called for no stain on the expensive dark woods with a beauty of their own (mahogany, cherry, and walnut), it looked favorably on coloring the light colored lesser woods: ash, birch, chestnut, elm, hickory, maple, oak, pine, and poplar.

Staining was often done to make the lesser woods look like the darker, more expensive ones. Walnut stains particularly have continued to be popular on some of the lighter woods.

Stain may still be desirable with some pieces. As already mentioned, it is often necessary with those that are left with patches of old coloration after stripping. Two woods that frequently have patches remaining in porous areas are birch and maple. For them a special category of wood coloring called *dye* stains is usually necessary. Not many colors are normally available, however. People living in towns or rural areas generally have to order it through the mail or know a cabinetmaker or refinisher who has some.

Other types of stain are more obtainable and come in a variety of colors to meet every need or fancy. You can definitely indulge yourself if you don't have to be concerned about resale value. If what you buy does represent a modest investment or is a hedge against inflation, however, you will probably want to take a conservative approach and either use no stain at all or one that is as light as possible. As a general rule, stay away from anything that has much red in it. If you are unsure of what to do, do some comparative shopping with stain colors in mind and notice just how much old furniture has no stain and how much is stained certain colors. Although there is more that can be said about using stain, it properly belongs in a book about how to do refinishing. A short bibliography of some excellent books on refinishing will be given at the end of this chapter.

Finishing

Old Finishes

The finish that is used to coat furniture is a necessary protection. It is a seal that is added to bare wood. One of its functions is to prevent air moisture from making the wood's surface rough by raising its grain. As a moisture barrier, a finish also prevents warpage, which can result if the wood swells. Another function of a finish is to keep the wood from absorbing dirt and stains. It also protects against abrasion and other physical damage.

In addition to protection, a finish also enhances the beauty of the wood. One of the ways it works is by penetrating its pores and reflecting their depth. The fuller revealing of depth makes the wood appear darker. Because some pores are filled more than others, contrasts result that give the wood its different grain patterns or figures. The application of finish also provides luster through the reflection.

The finishes used on old furniture, for the most part, were different from today's. In a way they were very sophisticated. Not the kind of sophistication that modern industrial chemists have developed by systematically varying dozens of formulas and applications, but the type that grew out of hundreds of years of trial and error by patient craftsmen in many different places of the world. Varnishes, the group of old finishes largest in number, had names that included Arabic, hauri, sandarach, Senegal, and Zanzibar.

Even though there were many different varieties of varnish, by far the most widely used finishes on old furniture were *paint* and *shellac*. They will be discussed at length, and briefer comments about varnish, lacquer, and tung oil will follow.

Old Paint

As a furniture finish, paint was mainly applied on the cheaper woods used in making country furniture. The finer woods were usually coated with shellac or other clear finishes. The chief ones that were painted were poplar and pine. Their grain patterns, generally considered unremarkable, could be opaquely covered and any surface defects concealed.

For furniture made of lesser woods, it was natural that paint be used again whenever a piece was refinished. It was not natural for pieces done originally with shellac, however, but many of them, including some very fine examples, got painted anyway. Some of the reasons that paint was used in refinishing were:

- Much of the furniture, however quaint, valuable or beautiful to us, grew tiresome to its owners. Changes in style occurred as today.
- The stripping methods available were unpleasant or dangerous—the use of strong lye or blowtorches, or scraping with knives or broken glass.
- Whereas stripping was so difficult, paint could quickly cover up dirt and wear and "freshen" a piece.
- Paint was more readily available than other finishes.
- Paint could conceal damage like stains, burns from irons, etc.

Some other things paint was used to cover were cracks, nails, lost veneer, inferior wood, and repairs. Although paint was used to hide problems, not every application was for concealment purposes. With pieces that were painted to begin with, a recoating with paint was the normal choice. It was not normal for those originally finished clear, however. Because paint was not their logical next coat, you should be a little more suspicious when buying them.

With either kind of piece, look carefully for uneven surfaces or any other detail that may be a clue to surface damage.

Although it is formidable by itself, the possibility of concealed damage is not the only problem of concern in buying painted furniture. The ease or difficulty with which the paint may be stripped also needs to be determined. The amount of hours or expense in stripping some painted pieces can mount up so greatly that it is hardly worth it to begin.

The hardest condition to contend with is, of course, many, many coats of paint over bare wood. The work is much easier if there is a good coat of shellac under the paint to act as a buffer, but ironically it is

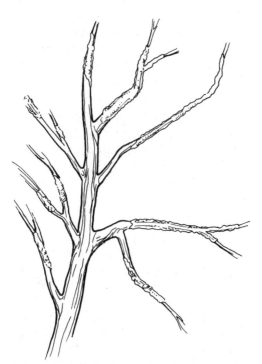

The raw material of shellac was secreted by insects on various tree parts. Pieces were broken off and carried to crude processing plants.

the pieces originally done with shellac, as already mentioned, that are more likely to have been painted to conceal damage. The best buys in painted furniture are pieces with just their original paint. Any damage on them can be seen and they are easy to strip.

Shellac

Shellac, or *spirit varnish* as it was called in earlier times, was the clear finish most frequently used on old furniture. It has been established that until about 1930 it was used by both factories and cabinetmakers over 90 percent of the time. Although almost completely replaced by lacquers and varnishes today, it still continues to be used whenever the very finest appearance is needed.

Shellac itself is derived from a resinlike secretion of an Asian insect, the *lac* bug. The secretion is deposited by the insect on tree bark, branches, and twigs. Twigs having some of the substance are broken off by natives and carried to primitive stone mills to begin a several-step process that ends with the finished product being mixed with alcohol to give it a suitable liquid form.

To the furniture finisher of the 1800s and later, shellac had several advantages. First of all it could produce a superior appearance through its ability to take a high polish when rubbed with a mixture of itself and linseed oil. Shellac was applied on the very finest pieces.

It was also applied on the very lowest items in a less sophisticated manner. Shellac's major benefit, as far as the factories were concerned, was its ability to dry rapidly and not gather dust. Shellac proved adaptable in other ways. At one point it was found that it could be combined with stain to create darker shades and reduce finishing steps. When spray equipment was developed, shellac was found to be adaptable to it.

Shellac remained in wide use until improved finishes, mainly lacquers, were invented. Despite its several advantages, it had always had the problem of not being water-resistant. With excessive moisture in the air it could easily turn cloudy white by absorbing some of the humidity.

In shopping for old furniture you will encounter many pieces made of oak and other light woods that appear brown. Some of this is due to stain, but more often it results from the aging of its shellac. If you have a desire to refinish a piece in its natural light color, it is important to know which kind of brown is involved. The kind that is found with aged shellac will disappear when stripped, but the type resulting from brown stain may remain in the wood. The best way to detect the presence of stain is to look for it on bare wood surfaces next to areas that were finished. The underneath part of legs is a good spot.

Shellac is easy to remove if it is not too thick. Thin layers can be cleaned away with alcohol and steel wool, but thicker coats need the greater solvent action of paint and varnish remover or dip-stripping. With dip-stripping, shellac comes off fairly fast with little disturbance to the wood. The presence of shellac under paint, as discussed earlier, makes stripping paint much easier.

Varnish

Varnish was never popular with the furniture factories. Because it contained some form of oil, it was slow to dry and attracted dust. Even though factories found it impractical, varnish was widely used by small furniture shops and by home handymen, especially in refinishing. For those who could deal with the dust problem, there were the practical benefits of its being harder and more water-resistant then shellac.

There was actually no single substance called varnish. As with paint, there were many varieties, each suited to a particular set of refinishing requirements. Up until the thirties most varnishes were made from oils mixed with tree gums and resins. The amount of oil involved varied with the use intended. *Short oil* varnishes, with a low proportion, were applied when a quick-drying, relatively hard material was needed. *Long oil* varieties, those with a higher than normal amount, dried slower but gave a more elastic protection less susceptible to temperature changes.

Although long oil varnishes dried to a less brittle consistency, when too much was applied, as with the short oil kinds, crackling was likely. It was said of old varnishes that:

> One coat never cracks,
> two coats seldom crack,
> three coats often crack,
> four coats always crack.

Today's varnishes, of which polyurethane is the most familiar, are made from synthetic, rather than natural substances. They are usually clearer and easier to apply and suffer less from the cracking problem. They are still very susceptible to dust in drying, however.

The varnish you are most likely to find on old furniture is *varnish stain*. Because it contained stain, it could be used to obscure an original shellac finish or to cover bare spots or any areas of damage. Besides paint it was the quickest way to refinish a piece. Varnish stain itself generally is easily stripped. In most cases the stain part will not have penetrated the wood.

A few nonstain, clear varnishes, not very many, were mavericks in their composition. If you run into a finish that is extremely difficult or impossible to strip, chances are it is an unusual type of varnish that may have to be scraped off. The same can also be said of certain kinds of paint. Paint is similar to varnish except for its pigments.

Linseed Oil

Linseed oil was a finish that had been used for centuries. It was generally replaced by shellac in the late 1800s. The longstanding advantage of linseed oil was a superior penetrating ability, which gave depth to wood grain and, in sufficient coats, could be built up to produce an attractive luster.

Boiled linseed oil was the kind used on furniture. It was faster drying than the raw oil, but even it had to be applied in very thin coats to prevent it from remaining sticky. To enable it to penetrate well and dry reasonably, the usual method was to apply it hot, wait a few minutes, then wipe up as much of the excess as possible. For an ordinary job, only about four coats were applied. To produce a full luster, many more were needed, and each had to be rubbed in between. As evidenced by the following old time schedule, some people got carried away in applying coats:

1 coat every day for a week,
1 coat every week for two weeks,
1 coat every two weeks for a month,
1 coat every month for a year,
1 coat every year thereafter.

Even without such extremes, linseed oil was not only beautiful, but also durable enough to resist abrasion and waterspotting. Except for its application time, it was a superior finish. Today linseed oil is still considered a good finish, but it lacks the drying and waterproofing qualities of tung oil.

By itself linseed oil is easy to strip. Frequently, however, it was combined with beeswax and the beeswax can present a problem.

Wax Finishes

Wax was often used on handmade country furniture. It was a quick finish and gave a nice appearance, but was not durable and never dried completely. It could be renewed by buffing, or applying another coat, however. In shopping you may see a piece that looks neither refinished nor quite as bare as freshly stripped; it may look washed out. In examining it, try to determine if it scrapes off like wax or has a waxy feel. If it does, and you decide to buy the piece and want to renew the wax, first clean it with Varsol, then apply one or two coats of ordinary paste wax. If you have a dark porous wood like walnut, try to buy a dark wax. A light one may show up in pores when it dries. You can use a hard wax like *carnauba* if you don't mind a lot of extra work.

If you decide that you don't want to do the periodic maintenance involved with a wax finish, there are the options of applying shellac or varnish. The first step is to do a complete job of removing as much of the wax as possible. Clean the piece several times with Varsol and steel wool followed by rags.

If the piece you have doesn't need the hardness and water resistance of varnish, you can use two or three coats of shellac (rubbed in between with fine sandpaper) and be done with it. If you prefer varnish, you will first need one coat of shellac to seal off any small residues of the wax. Without the coat of shellac, the wax will prevent the varnish from drying or produce in its surface small cratered specks called *fisheyes*. Do not use tung oil over shellac unless you desire a high gloss.

Lacquer

The first lacquers were actually varnishes developed from the sap of sumac trees in China and Japan. The name *lacquer* was taken from the *lac* tree, the major source of the sap. The making of Oriental lacquer was a complex process and its application a highly developed art. Lacquer was generally used on both wood and metal to produce a very high polish. Some very valuable pieces of Chinese lacquerware—boxes, trays, etc., were finished over a period of five to twenty years.

The modern lacquers that began to be developed in the twenties were similar to the Oriental only in their high polish; otherwise they were completely different. Rather than being derived from natural substances, the new lacquers were the product of industrial chemistry and research. Their full name was *pyroxylin nitro cellulose* lacquers. Their main component was cellulose fibers (mainly cotton) treated with nitric acid. It was almost always applied by spray gun.

Industrially produced lacquer was used to finish some furniture in the thirties, but it is not likely that you will find it until you get into forties pieces. Lacquer strips fairly easily with either paint and varnish remover or dip-stripping.

Tung Oil

Tung oil, like linseed oil, penetrates the wood. Its penetrating capacity brings out the wood's depth with less appearance of something added—it emphasizes wood rather than polish. Tung oil is mentioned here because it is one of the materials you are likely to use if you do any refinishing.

Tung oil was originally used in China and for a time was known here as *Chinawood oil*. Although it was not widely used on American furniture until recently, it is an extremely good finish in terms of beauty, drying time, and waterproofing. It is not as waterproof as polyurethane varnish, however, coat for coat.

Tung oil is seldom sold in its pure form. It is usually mixed with other oils and some type of varnish resin is included. In one form or another, tung oil is probably the most widely used substance in the antiques trade. Although its main appeal is its ease of application, some of the better tung oil products are not a compromise in other respects. Dupont 704C, Penetrating Oil Sealer and Finish, for instance, combines tung oil with a very hard varnish ingredient, *phenolic resin*. Its price and the price of most other tung oil finishes is considerably lower than that of those sold in hardware and department stores in those neat wooden display cases. Most refinishing products are much cheaper, in fact, if you do a little shopping at paint, hardware and building supply stores.

Rubbing Down

Rubbing down is the last step in refinishing. Its purposes are to smooth the finish and sometimes to adjust its sheen. Rubbing down is accomplished by using one of several varieties of abrasives together with a lubricant that softens its action. The quickest abrasive to use in smoothing is very fine (number 4/0) steel wool. For a lubricant, use creme polish or any odorless oil. Vegetable oil will work well. The process is carried out by using enough oil with the steel wool to prevent dry rubbing.

To avoid going through the finish, strokes are made with the grain of the wood and with light to medium pressure. The steel wool must be spread out in your hand well enough to avoid rubbing that is too concise. It is important to be conservative in rubbing edges and high spots where a normal pressure would remove too much finish.

When rubbing is complete, the entire piece can be cleaned with Varsol, then either left alone or rubbed again with a cloth and just a light coat of oil or creme polish.

Refinishing Combination Furniture

Combination furniture, any of several types composed of both solid wood and veneers, usually cannot be refinished with the methods applied to other types of construction. One main reason is that, because of its veneer, it is a poor candidate for the usual hot tank method of dip-stripping. It can be stripped successfully using a cold tank but, as mentioned earlier, the cost is greater and the process is not available in many localities.

Because it avoids a water rinse (as is used even with the cold tank), hand-stripping is the safest and best method for stripping combination furniture. Although it is in a different category because you usually do the work yourself, the cost for hand-stripping is generally less, and you can control the quality to a greater degree. With combination furniture the work is usually not too difficult, especially when there is just a clear coat of shellac, varnish, or lacquer to remove. Veneer is not affected by

most home paint and varnish removers. Only the water rinse types can do damage because they require hosing down the softened finish.

Besides stripping, another concern with combination furniture is what kind of finish to use once stripping and other preparation measures are taken. The basic problem in the finishing stage is to try to match the shade and color of the veneer with that of the solid wood parts. The solid wood, once the original finish is removed, is usually lighter than the veneer and usually has a different grain. Essentially there are three finishes used to deal with the situation — *shading lacquer*, *varnish stain*, and *stain and finish*. Those who have spray equipment use shading lacquer (lacquer containing stain). It is finish that is essentially applied to bare wood and is followed by a clear lacquer. Shading lacquer was the original factory method for combination furniture. It is still considered the best for refinishing because the shade can be increased by applying more and more spray.

If you use the shading lacquer approach, your biggest problem may be finding spray materials to do the job. Large city paint stores sometimes have the ingredients, but more often will only have aerosol cans. A local refinisher or cabinet shop might advise you on where to get materials if you cannot find them elsewhere. Aerosol cans, although seemingly expensive, are often more economical for the amateur refinisher doing just a few pieces. You can also do a professional job with them after a little reading and practice.

The second general method of refinishing combination furniture is the use of *varnish stain*. Many people that don't have a spray gun resort to it. Today the primary type used is polyurethane varnish containing stain. Although not up to the standard of shading lacquer, it can do a good job if it is applied well. The new foam brushes help to apply the finish more smoothly than those made with bristles and are available along with varnish stain at many paint and hardware stores. Reading up on the use of varnish is suggested if you go this route. Dust is a big obstacle, and knowing how to minimize it is important. Knowing how to apply varnish to prevent streaks, runs, and other complications is important also.

The third finishing approach for combination furniture is the set of ordinary home methods used in refinishing wood furniture that is completely solid. A large number of combination items were made with mahogany for many of the solid parts as well as the veneer and can look very good done with just a clear finish such as tung oil. Other pieces of lesser value that were veneered with walnut or mahogany, but used gum or birch solids, can be at least tolerable using a clear finish.

Although it is less than ideal, some people have produced a respectable finish using stain for the birch or gum parts while leaving the veneer natural. The stain often takes poorly, but it does darken the solid wood enough to make it approach the shade of the veneer. Some sort of stain, whether mixed with finish or just in the ordinary wipe-on form that is separate, is especially desirable when there is a significant amount of old stain left in the wood after stripping. The condition is more acute when the original stain was red mahogany. Red stain usually produces more contrast with the natural color of the wood than does any shade of brown.

Books on Repair and Refinishing

Hand, Jackson. *How to Do Your Own Wood Finishing*. New York: Harper and Row, 1976. Available in paperback.

Kinney, Ralph Parsons. *The Complete Book of Furniture Repair and Refinishing*. New York: Scribner's, 1971.

Savage, Jessie D. *Professional Furniture Refinishing for the Amateur*. New York: Harper and Row, 1975. Available in paperback.

Jones, Thomas H. *Furniture Fix and Finish Guide*. Reston, Va: Reston Publishing Co. (Prentice-Hall), 1980.

8

Furniture Woods

Wood has been the overwhelming choice for furniture for thousands of years. No other material has even approached the combination of characteristics that make it so adaptable for furniture. No *natural* material that is nearly as light as wood comes close to being as strong. The abundance of wood has always made it cheap and convenient. The use of wood probably began with the invention of simple scraping tools made of stone. As finer tools were developed, its almost infinite capacity for cutting, carving, drilling, and other processes were realized.

Although the practical features of wood were enough for it to become the traditional medium for furniture, its beauty put it even further above other materials. It is interesting to note that the plastics used in much of today's articles are stained and molded to simulate wood's colors and grain patterns. The imitation is not merely for tradition. Wood colors are warm. Combined with the natural luster that wood develops with age, they create a soft, harmonizing glow that can be almost sublimely cozy. The beauty of wood's grain patterns add more richness.

Identifying Woods

There are approximately a hundred species of wood in the world used for furniture. About twenty of them, mainly those that are native, have been used widely in the United States. Although identifying a comparatively small number would seem fairly simple, there are several confusing things that make it difficult:

- There are gross similarities between several species.

- Trees within the same species are somewhat different, due to growing conditions and inheritance.
- There are several ways to cut wood, each yielding a different appearance.
- The appearance is further changed as wood is made into furniture and then finished.
- Wood changes with age, becoming more mellow and usually darker.
- Much fakery has occurred through staining one wood to resemble a more costly one.

Wood Anatomy

Although there is a considerable basis for confusion, most woods can be identified given some basic information and some features to compare. This section will offer some basic facts about trees in general and the features that need comparison. A large section later on will include more specifics

for each species. For some species a written description, while helpful, will not be enough, and several comparisons of actual wood will be necessary. A few may require the help of someone familiar with them.

In America trees are divided into two groups, *hardwoods* and *softwoods*. The division is somewhat arbitrary, however; some of the hardwoods are soft and some of the softwoods are hard. The hardwood label technically stands for the group of trees with broad leaves, while the softwood name somewhat inaccurately designates the trees with needles and cones. In other countries more accurate terms are used.

No matter how much they differ, all trees are similar in their basic structure. A cross-section of almost any tree would look something like the illustration. Most obvious in the diagram are *growth rings*, the concentric circles. Each spring, as a tree begins its growth phase, it adds a fresh, generally light-colored layer of very porous material that assists in a rapid flow of sap

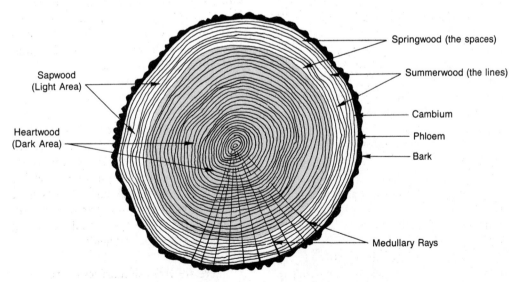

A cross-section of a tree showing its basic anatomy.

up to its newly forming stems and leaves. When enough of this new *springwood* is completed and the new foliage formed, the tree begins producing *summerwood*, which usually is darker, denser, and stronger than the spring growth.

The shaded inner section of the diagram, the *heartwood*, consists of rings of old growth that have been chemically transformed. Chemical changes have darkened and strengthened them to provide a more rigid core of support for the tree. The lighter outer portion of rings, the *sapwood*, is newer growth that is still active in transporting sap. Each ring, in turn, will become part of the heartwood. The heartwood, because it is harder, is the one generally chosen for furniture.

Pores and other vessels in the sapwood rings carry sap upward from the roots. The downward transport system coming from the leaves is contained in the *phloem*, the light area immediately next to the bark. One of the most significant tree parts is the *cambium*. It is a tiny layer of cells between the phloem and the outermost growth ring. The cambium is the tree's growth medium. New rings are made by its cells.

The spokelike lines in the lower portion of the figure represent *medullary rays*. Their function is to carry sap *across* the growth rings and to store excess food. The presence of medullary rays on a board's surface can be very striking. *Quartersawing*, the usual process for revealing them, has to aim each cut at or near the center of a tree in order to capture rays on board facings. Wood that is sawn with rays showing is highly warp-resistant.

Wood Comparisons

Although differentiating wood species can be confusing there are two areas of comparison, besides color, that make it somewhat easier. One is pore distribution. Pores, when concentrated, are found only in the springwood rings where they provide a rapid sap transport. Ash, hickory, and chestnut have this feature. Most other woods with pores have them in the summerwood also. A few woods — cherry, maple, and poplar — have pores that are difficult to see unless the wood is stained. Pine and all other softwoods, technically speaking, do not have pores. Their sap transport vessels, called *vascular bundles*, are, for all practical purposes, invisible. Consider the following:

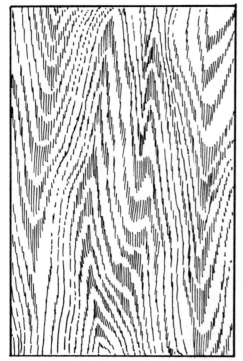

Some trees have pores only in their obvious spring-wood rings. They provide a very rapid transport of sap early in the spring. In other trees the summer-wood rings are the darker ones.

Obvious and Concentrated Pores	Obvious and Diffuse Pores
Ash	Birch
Chestnut	Mahogany
Hickory	Oak
	Walnut

Barely Visible Pores	No Pores Per Se
Cherry	Pine and
Maple	Other
Poplar	Softwoods

The second useful guide to identifying a wood is through the prominance of its rings. Some species can be distinguished according to whether their rings are distinct of faint.

Distinct Rings	Faint Rings
All Softwoods	Maple
Ash	Poplar
Chestnut	
Elm	
Hickory	
Oak	

Other categories for comparison, especially color, will be discussed with the individual species (next).

Individual Wood Species

Ash

According to results from the Department of Agriculture's Forest Products Laboratory, only two American hardwoods, cherry and oak, are above ash in woodworking ease using modern power tools. Ash is on par with the likes of *chestnut*, *maple*, and *walnut*. In durability and strength it compares with any species.

Ash is naturally a light-colored wood that is *ring porous*: Its springwood rings contain large and distinct pores. Its summerwood, which has only very faint pores, is cream-colored and smooth. Overall, ash resembles chestnut. From a distance it also looks like oak, but up close its lack of summerwood pores reveals the difference.

In earlier times ash was mainly employed for strength and durability. It was frequently used to make tool handles, wheel spokes, oars, baseball bats, butter churns, and ice boxes. Many agricultural articles were made with it. Today a considerable amount of ash is sold for export to countries where it is more popular than in the United States.

Either by itself or in combination with other species, ash was an eminent chair wood. It made strong legs, spindles, and other supporting parts. In colonial days many Windsor chairs had ash parts. In the golden oak era, chairs made entirely of ash were sold by Sears and Montgomery Ward.

Birch

The use of birch in old furniture was usually for economic reasons. Strength, hardness, and resiliency were not sacrificed, however — birch is outstanding in those properties. Most frequently it can be found in lathe-turned chair parts: spindles, legs, and stretchers. Many items of reproduction furniture have birch parts.

Yellow and sweet birch are the main species used in furniture, and both range from yellow to red to brown. Whichever species is observed, the wood varies greatly in its texture and figure. Its pores, which are open to a degree, create an irregular-looking texture because of their differing sizes and arrangements. Birch's figures (grain patterns) vary enough that elements of it often resemble other woods. Because of the resemblance, birch is somewhat difficult to identify in old furniture. Usually it has been stained to look like cherry, mahogany, or walnut. In most cases it has a heavy coat of finish to obscure its irregular grain.

Cherry

This wood, which comes from the wild black cherry tree of deep forests, is one of the world's finer hardwoods. In tests conducted by the U.S.D.A. Forest Products Laboratory, it scored significantly higher in ease of machining than any other American species.

The color of cherry is an outstanding characteristic. When fresh-sawn it varies from light tan or pink in younger trees to darker shades in others that are more mature. With age it darkens further and ranges from brownish to purplish red. Under age-darkened shellac it is even deeper in color. The traditional preference with cherry is for the darker shades.

Because the color of cherry is its main visible feature, and because there is a wide range of it to copy, woods stained to resemble it often pass on their color merits alone. Due to its similar grain, hardness, and luster, maple makes the best wood to fake cherry, although poplar is used more often because it is cheaper and easier to work with. Occasional grain patterns in birch so resemble cherry that it also has been used as an imposter.

Cherry has usually been a cabinetmaker's wood rather than one used in mass production. It was often used in country furniture, in the simple elegant work of the Shakers, and in much of the finer furniture of the Victorian era, Eastlake in particular.

Chestnut

In 1904 a fungus accidentally imported from Europe began attacking the chestnut trees in a small section of New York state. Although efforts were made to control it, in just a few years the blight had spread throughout the entire United States and killed virtually every chestnut tree. Even today a fresh-planted seedling can only grow to a few feet before falling prey to the still surviving fungus.

The holes that typify wormy chestnut lumber are a bit misleading. They are not the cause of the trees' death but the result. Many dying trees become subject to boring insects that eat and tunnel the wood in all directions.

Very little furniture was made with wormy chestnut. The antique chestnut furniture available on today's market was made before the blight. The wormy articles you may see are either new ones that have had an overlying veneer removed. Wormy chestnut was the underlayment of a lot of furniture covered with oak veneer. After becoming inundated with worm holes, chestnut was considered second-class.

The original unblighted chestnut was made into attractive bedroom furniture and tables in the middle 1800s. Sometimes it was used with other woods, especially walnut. In chests of drawers it can usually be detected by the distinctive dovetailing of its drawers, which appears as a column of pegged half-circles.

Unblighted chestnut is a clean-looking wood with pores concentrated only in its springwood. It bears a close resemblance to ash, but can be distinguished by its lighter weight.

Elm

Elm is easy to identify. One way to recog-

Half-moon dovetailing on a drawer of chestnut furniture.

nize it is by its pore arrangement: pores in elm appear to mesh sideways. The pattern is said to resemble the small breast markings of a partridge. In addition to its peculiar meshing, elm has a characteristic figure. Although fairly straight and regular in most boards, the figure usually resorts to meandering swirls and zigzags somewhere on other board surfaces.

Many of the dealers who specialize in refinished or stripped oak furniture frequently sell elm pieces, especially chairs. In the golden oak era, elm was associated with oak because it could be finished to look the same color. In a 1908 Sears catalog, most of the pressed-back chairs, the ones with machine-imprinted carvings, were elm or mostly elm.

Elm reputedly makes the best chair bottoms. Because of its interlocking grain, it doesn't split like most woods. Early craftsmen, knowing this, used elm for wheel hubs, chopping blocks, and the heads of large mallets used to join heavy beams. Some of the best Windsor chairs had elm seats.

Hickory

There are sixteen species and twenty varieties of this wood in North America. *Shagbark hickory*, the most important for furniture, is characterized by a brown to reddish-brown heartwood and a cream-colored sapwood. Wood from both parts have been used in furniture. Sometimes considered an "ironwood," hickory has a peak combination of traits of sturdiness: It is hard, strong, tough, stiff, and resilient in the highest combination of any American wood. The best means to identify it are its large, long, and open pores, which are obvious on any board or round furniture part.

Because hickory worked well for steam-bending and for parts needing sure strength, some of the finest chairs were made of it. Even in small thicknesses it was sufficient for chair slats, spindles, and other parts. Windsor chairs combined hickory with other native hardwoods to produce what is now perhaps the most sought-after single American antique.

In country-made chairs, hickory spindles were often joined to chair bottoms using a *greenwood method*. First the spindles, thoroughly dried, were made bulbous on one end, while the chair bottom, made of green wood of another species, was carved with tightly fitting sockets. Once the spindles were driven and the bottom dried, the joints were very secure. Many of them are still holding.

Maple

Maple is the hardest wood *ordinarily* used in furniture. The tree it comes from is sometimes called the *rock maple*, although more often it is known as the *sugar maple* because of the sugar and syrup it provides. Someone described the wood of the maple as having "all the colors of biscuits." The description applies well to the changes maple goes through as it matures: When fresh-cut it is a very pale beige, but as it ages it approaches orange with a reddish tinge.

Maple was often stained a reddish orange to simulate age. Other cheaper woods, especially poplar, were given the aged maple color. During a period of great walnut zeal, considerable maple was stained a dark brown color to resemble walnut. In other times it was colored to simulate cherry or mahogany.

Maple is similar to cherry in several important respects. Like cherry it has very faint, closed pores, Somehow the pore structure provides a high surface toughness that, incidentally, makes both woods the first choices for cutting boards. Other common features include a relatively faint figure and the ability to take a high polish.

The high density of maple's surface makes it easy to dip-strip unless it has been stained to simulate one of the more prestigious dark woods. Because maple requires a deeply penetrating stain, almost all attempts to remove it leave some of the stain in the wood. A dark red mahogany is the worst.

Maple has two interesting abnormalities — curly maple and birdseye maple. The former looks like many curled fragments imbedded in the wood. Birdseye also is appropriately labeled. The eyes in it are about ⅛ to ¼ inch in diameter and are randomly scattered. It has been speculated that the eyes are mutant buds that have grown within the tree. Another interesting pattern in maple results with quartersawn wood. The fairly uniform stripes, the medullary rays that are made visible, are referred to as *fiddleback* or *tigerstripe* maple. The quartersawing process is explained near the end of this chapter.

Mahogany

There are several important species of this wood. One, *Honduras mahogany*, has been considered the world's premier furniture wood since the 1600s. A second, *African mahogany*, has often been substituted for it because of a general resemblance. Honduras mahogany is not limited to one country but is found in much of Central America, in northern South America, and on many Caribbean islands. Explorers from Europe returned home with it as early as the 1500s. Because of its finer texture and ease of working with hand tools, it gradually replaced oak in England as the wood for fine furniture.

In America mahogany was the chief wood used in fine furniture until about 1840. Thereafter it was replaced by walnut and rosewood. Today, articles of solid mahogany are sought widely by collectors and are usually very expensive. Some pieces made with veneer, however, are still available at moderate prices.

African mahogany, of which there is more than one species, was discovered early as a substitute for Honduras. Except for a slight coarseness and a tendency for some of its pores to cluster, the better grades have often passed as the more favored wood.

Both Honduras and African mahogany are tan or pink when freshly cut. With age they darken to varying shades of reddish brown or copper. Furniture bleached by sunlight becomes a light reddish tan. A considerable amount of mahogany is stained, however, the practice going back to the eighteenth century when Thomas Chippendale began using linseed oil and brick dust to finish mahogany pieces. The dark red stains used in most mahogany reproductions to simulate the Chippendale effect are tough to remove totally.

Many of the reproductions made during the twenties and later are stylized versions of some of the older items made during the 1700s and 1800s. Many of them have mahogany veneers, especially from some of the cheaper species. One important mahogany substitute, *sapele*, usually shows a bold striped feature. The striping is visible on a lot of reproductions.

Oak

There are over fifty species of oak in the

United States alone. The most practical way of dividing them is according to color. The ones that have a slightly red tone in lightly colored furniture are *red oak*. The ones with a wheat-colored tan are *white oak*.

There are two kinds of pores in oak, and both are large. The ones in the springwood are open and give oak its partially rough texture. The other kind are filled with a substance called *lignin* and produce a smooth surface. The lignin pores are distributed throughout both the summerwood and the springwood. In the springwood they often overlap the open pores.

Oak was the dominant furniture wood of the American colonies, as it has been in England for centuries. Its use diminished only after mahogany was found superior in woodworking ease. Usually only country craftsmen who were distant from suppliers of imported woods and the compelling fashion of the cities continued to use it.

Not until the nineteenth century, during the Victorian Age, did oak regain some of its prominence. Its widespread use in factory furniture of the golden oak era followed a brief period during which art furniture of oak was constructed and ornately carved by hand. Hand-crafted oak had been of high fashion and expensive. The golden oak industry, which began in the 1870s, eventually enabled millions to own stylized versions of the earlier handmade pieces through its efficient production methods and machinery.

While the golden oak continued on through the depression, another style, mission furniture, utilized oak in forms that were especially sturdy and rectangular.

Oak was the only wood ever to be quartersawn in great numbers. A high incidence of quartered oak in the golden oak style resulted from the newfound ease with which the wood itself could be sawn to display its rays. It stood as a tour-de-force for the new technology. Today oak rays revealed by the process are considered beautiful by some, but only diplomatically interesting by others. The general preference is for small and subtle ones that produce a delicate radiance.

Pine

Until recent years pine was almost entirely a country furniture wood. In the practical country style it was used primarily for tables, chests, hutches, corner cupboards, and kitchen furniture. Very often it was considered a lesser wood and was painted.

Pine is easily identified by the sharp contrast between its light and dark rings. Its lack of pores heightens the difference.

There are two general kinds of pine — hard and soft. The hard species are the southern pines: *longleaf, shortleaf, slash*, and *loblolly*. The hard ones give better results in dip-stripping. The wood does not fur up as it does in the soft pines. The soft species, generally from the north and west, include *sugar* and *western white pine*. Most consider the soft species more pleasing in grain pattern and color. The hard ones are more durable.

Although their colors vary, most other softwoods have the same sharp contrast between springwood and summerwood as pine. Because of a relative scarcity of hardwoods in the west, more furniture made there is of softwood.

Poplar

Poplar was one of the most widespread woods in old furniture. The use of it probably began with very early country articles.

In the middle nineteenth century it was used by factories in the different kinds of cottage furniture. Later it became the wood of many stylized Victorian pieces made notably in the Grand Rapids renaissance designs. Many of the hidden structural parts in a great variety of old items were made of poplar.

Except that it generally provides a nice finish, poplar is not a fine wood. Other than for its use with golden oak it was usually painted or darkly stained. Although it is considered a hardwood because of its tree's broad leaves, it is actually very soft, probably the softest in general use for furniture. While its grain is pleasing, the color of poplar varies considerably. Basically it is yellow or yellowish green but may also have brown, black, or purple streaks (which sometimes show up after stripping painted country pieces).

Poplar is a favorite today despite its inadequacies. Many articles of poplar are sold already dip-stripped. Dip-stripping gives it a favorable appearance when oxalic acid is used as a brightening agent. Unless darkly streaked wood is present, the appearance of such poplar is one of the lightest and most homogeneous found in old furniture.

Because of its negligible pores, poplar is relatively easy to strip. It does present a problem, however, because of its softness. Like pine, it tends to fur up in most dip-stripping processes. The furring, unless severe, can usually be countered by light to moderate sanding, however.

Poplar is the wood most frequently used to counterfeit cherry and walnut. It takes stain exceptionally well and if the color is accurate many a novice furniture buyer is fooled by its appearance. There are some easily recognizable differences, however, to prevent being misled. Both cherry and walnut are much heavier than poplar. Cherry is more radiant and has a more distinct figure; walnut has visible pores.

Walnut

Walnut is considered by most to be America's finest wood. Perhaps no other wood is as charismatic. Part of the high regard is due to walnut's dark color. Another aspect is its ease of woodworking: It machines beautifully, shapes well by hand, and can be carved to very exacting detail. Just as significant is the luster that most of the time can be developed in refinishing it.

Walnut has pores in both its springwood and summerwood. Usually they are medium in coarseness. An old process of finishing walnut included the use of fillers to close the pores to provide more sheen. Several layers of plain shellac was the usual method, however.

Although it is generally dark, walnut varies considerably in color. When fresh-sawn, it is like cocoa, sometimes even having a bluish tint. With age it darkens to different intensities of brown. A special variety identified as *Virginia walnut* is quite red.

Most quality walnut is *leaf-figured* or finely *striped*. A great deal, though, is mixed, some boards even showing medullary rays.

Walnut and mahogany are often similar in appearance, especially in old furniture bleached by sunlight. The resemblance was a significant factor in walnut's supplanting mahogany in the early nineteenth century for art furniture. Many uncompromisingly fine period pieces were made of walnut beginning about 1810.

Walnut was most popular in the Victorian Age. No other wood except oak was used as widely and with so much variation.

Several grades and styles of walnut furniture were available for every room in the house. Country furniture was at its best when made with it.

Other Woods

Basswood

Also referred to as *whitewood* or *linden*, basswood is the softest and lightest hardwood used for furniture parts. With a fine texture and straight grain, it is easy to work with both machine and hand tools and warps very little. Basswood is the wood of choice for architectural drawing boards. Its main use in old furniture, because of its softness, was usually in making drawer parts, cabinet backings, and other nonvisible components. During the 1920s and 1930s it became an important substitute for the gumwoods used in making combination furniture (see Gum, below).

Beech

Although beech was used in fine furniture in Europe, it has, for some strange reason, never been popular in this country until the recent emphasis on naturally finished modern furniture. Beech is uniform in appearance, with a key distinction of having a profusion of many brown flecks up to ⅛ inch long. The flecks are said to be something like medullary rays. Although beech is found in many items of kitchenware, it is likely that with old furniture you will only see it in bentwood chairs, European antiques, and a few pieces of middle modern furniture.

Ebony

Although there are over a hundred species of ebony, it is rare enough today so that usually only veneer is employed in furniture. Even in olden times it was seldom used except as inlay borders on small chests and boxes or on the very finest pianos. Some ebony that is not entirely black looks like a dark version of rosewood. In the Victorian era, furniture made of ebony held the very highest rank. The ebony-looking pieces that are on the old furniture market today are, in almost every case, made from any of several species that were *ebonized* with the use of black stain or black paint.

Gum

Gum, either *red* or *black*, is a soft, fine-textured wood that takes stain well and, combined with a stain in the finish, is very convincing. Because of its stain capacity it was widely used in the twenties and thirties in combination with walnut and mahogany veneers. Gum was employed for all but the flat veneered sections. It continues to be used today in low- and moderate-priced articles.

Mixed Hardwoods

This phrase or another one, *northern hardwoods*, was applied to wood that was used with items of furniture made with any or several of the less-popular species. Some of the species were beech, soft maple, gum, birch, and sycamore. In most cases any differences in appearance were covered up by using a finish containing a dark stain. Sometimes this was done on the basis that different species are better for different furniture parts. It continues to be done with many types of furniture.

Rosewood

Rosewood, which is mainly from Brazil, is a strong, hard wood that takes a high polish in spite of having coarse pores. Its colors are somewhat complex. The background is a warm reddish brown with lighter random patches of golden or violet brown. Black streaks run throughout. One of the world's most esteemed woods, rosewood is found on the finest old pianos, on billiard tables, fine cabinets, dressing tables, and étagères. You may encounter it in something less costly, usually as veneer.

Wood Processes

Sawing Lumber and Board Appearance

Most lumber, the great bulk of it, is *parallel-sawn* as in the illustration. This is by far the easiest sawing method. After a log is placed on a saw mill platform, its waste removed, and its sides made square or rectangular, the remaining wood is successively sawn into boards having the same thickness. While the thicknesses are the same, the appearance of each board differs considerably and has but a general pattern to compare with others.

There are two general patterns for parallel-sawn lumber. One, a *striped figure*, results from cutting a tree along its center or parallel to it. The striped pattern results because the saw cut is closely perpendicular to the growth rings and shows them at their narrowest. In the second general figure, *leaf* or *slash* grain, the angle of cut is greater, and the rings appear larger and as irregular elliptical segments.

A pure striped figure is rare. Most board faces show either a mixture of the two figures or just slash grain alone. The bias

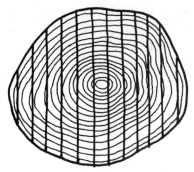

Parallel-sawn lumber.

is toward slash grain, largely because of variations in tree shape: Seldom do trees grow perfectly round or straight. Another factor leading to slash grain is the slightly tapered shape of tree trunks. The taper leads to a slight angle of cut when a log is presented to the saw blade.

A third kind of figure is produced by a process called *quarter sawing*. The method is used with several woods having prominent and attractive medullary rays. Because medullary rays originate from the center of a tree like spokes of a wheel, they are re-

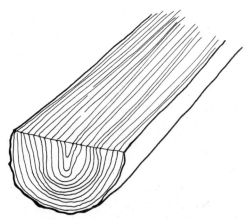

Striped pattern sawn from a perpendicular cut on an almost perfectly straight tree.

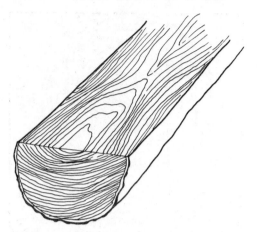

Slash cut producing oval segments. Oval segments also arise from perpendicular cuts to a nonperfect tree.

Rotary veneer cutting. Irregular segments are produced.

vealed by any saw cut aimed at the center. Occasionally boards having these rays are produced by chance in the usual parallel method of sawing, which takes the tree as it comes to the blade. Quartersawing, one variety of which is shown in the illustration, enables many more boards with rays to be sawn from a single tree by changing the angle of cut.

Veneer

Besides regular sawn lumber, there is veneer. Centuries ago veneer began to be

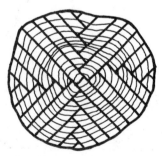

Quartersawing. Boards are cut approximately like spokes from a wheel.

utilized as a way of "stretching" rare and valuable woods. *Parallel sawing*, the first method for producing it, usually yielded only thick cuts of wood. Because the sawing also meant considerable waste, more efficient methods were developed. The technique of *slicing*, which began sometime in the 1800s, is still used today as the main method for producing furniture veneers. Thicknesses of $\frac{1}{40}$ inch or less are possible.

The method itself, which leaves very little waste, utilizes a heavy knife blade, close alignment of the log to be cut, and enough blade speed to prevent splintering. The result, as with veneer sawing, produces figures that are the same as if the wood were made into boards.

Rotary veneer cutting, the most recent method of producing veneer, produces very different figures. As shown in the illustration, the rotary process produces veneer from around a tree rather than in parallel cuts along its length. The result is a figure showing *fragments* of the tree's rings. Because of its irregular figure, rotary veneer was seldom used in old furniture. Occasionally it can be found on the side sections of inexpensive oak and poplar cabinet pieces made after about 1900.

The veneer used in old furniture was usually made from fancy figures of wood. The figure with the most charisma is *burl*. Found in walnut, elm, poplar, and redwood, burl looks like small knots with other irregularities surrounding them. Burl is sliced from peculiar mounds occurring unpredictably on the trunks of some trees. Some say the mounds are the tree's own repairs to points of injury. *Crotch* veneer, often confused with burl, is taken from tree sections where the trunk divides or where limbs branch out. The figure often resembles a radiating flame with denser wood at its center. Veneer taken from *stump wood* may resemble either burl or crotch or both.

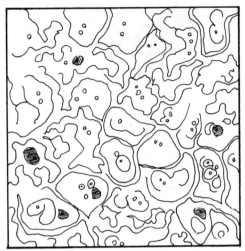

Burl veneer. Burl is said to be a tree's response to points of injury.

Seasoning and Kiln Drying

Most of the sap in live trees is water. Normally the water is contained in individual cells and causes their walls to expand. Once a tree is sawn, the water begins moving from the cells to the outside air by capillary action. Evaporation occurs as the water surfaces. Air then moves into the vacant cells and the wood becomes lighter. As the cell walls relax, the wood begins to shrink and becomes stronger.

The traditional way of drying wood is called *seasoning*. The method basically involves stacking fresh-sawn lumber in layers separated by small pieces of wood called *stickers*. The stickers allow air to circulate to speed drying. Warpage is prevented by the weight of succeeding layers. Seasoning takes several months and is complete when moisture within the wood is approximately equal to the outside air.

The precise measurement of wood moisture is an integral part of *kiln drying*, the more modern process of drying wood. In kiln drying, stickered lumber is placed in a large, sealed chamber where air circulation, temperature, and humidity are varied in gradual steps until equilibrium or an-

Crotch veneer. Sawn from places where tree limbs come together. Frequently confused with burl.

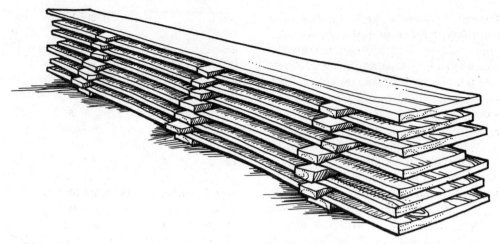

Stickered lumber. The stickers allow air circulation. This is the oldest method of seasoning lumber.

other desirable point of moisture content is reached. Although expensive, kiln drying has the advantages of speed, evenness, and thoroughness. The great majority of today's furniture wood is kiln-dried. In most instances, however, wood is placed in a kiln only after several months of seasoning.

Seasoning in olden times had none of the advantages of kiln-drying. The only insurance for adequate drying was patience and time.

Shrinkage that turned up after the construction of an item was due to incomplete seasoning and can be found frequently in country and other handmade furniture. Gaps between doors and doorframes and spaces between joined boards are not unusual. The great majority of factory furniture, on the other hand, is relatively free of seasoning failures.

Wood Deterioration

There are several kinds of wood deterioration that affect furniture; warpage is probably the most frequent. It is brought on by excessive moisture or dryness, a combination of both, or by twisted grain patterns within the wood. The main kind of warpage is technically called *cupping*. Cupping occurs when one side of a board has significantly more moisture than the other. The condition can often be found on tabletops that are too thin or on those that were not covered with finish on their bottom side.

Cupping is the kind of warpage that occurs across the grain. When one side of a board becomes excessively wet, its pores become swollen and begin to crowd each other. Because the middle of the board absorbs more water, it becomes the peak point of warpage. The bulged side is always the wet side. A typical cupped board is shown in the illustration.

There is another factor in cupping besides the wetness-dryness differential. It has to do with the dimensions of the wood. Wood that is thick enough, relative to its width, contains itself against cupping.

Boards that are thin and relatively wide, conversely, are the main victims of cupping. A piece of thin veneer is the most vulnerable and will go into a coil when one side is wet. A 2 by 4, on the other hand, although it may distort in other ways, will never cup. According to the U.S.D.A. Forest Products Laboratory, the possibility of a board's cupping is predictable given its dimensions. The maximum width for a 1-inch-thick board to prevent cupping, the laboratory says, is 8 inches, and the same ratio applies roughly to other dimensions.

The ratio given is for loose lumber. Furniture boards that are glued together or otherwise secured are stabilized beyond the 1-inch-to-8-inch ratio. Cupping is frequent, however, on old tabletops with wide boards made of soft woods fastened down with nails. Nails do not usually hold well in soft woods.

The general term for wood deterioration that occurs outdoors is *weathering*. Wood left outside is exposed to nature's cycles of day and night, its seasons, and its changing weather. Sunlight bleaches it and turns it gray; rain water swells it; heat from the sun causes it to shrink. *Checking*, a series of small cracks and splits on the wood's surface, results from the sun's heat producing a shrinkage that is too rapid. Weathering also occurs indoors to a lesser extent. One of the main purposes of a varnish or other finish is to prevent its damage.

A serious kind of wood deterioration is caused by fungus. The term *dry rot* comes

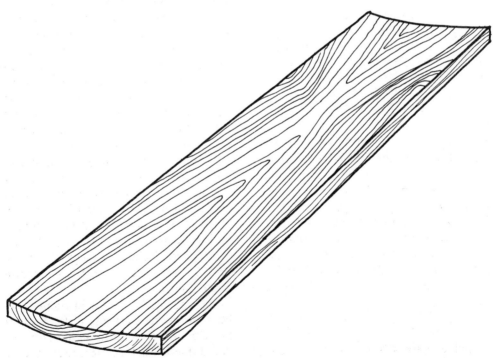

A cupped board. Results from unequal moisture absorption. The wetter side is the bulged side.

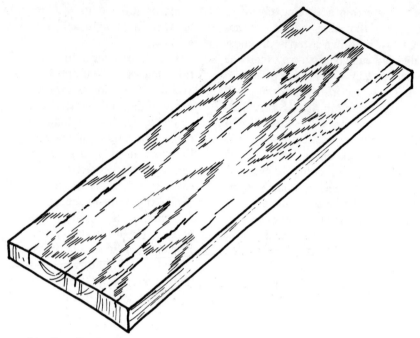

Checking **consists of small splits on the face of a board. It usually results from a too-rapid drying process.**

from looking at the *results* of fungus decay, but the organisms actually only work under wet conditions. Their damage is often done on furniture feet that have stood on wet dirt.

Insects are also a serious threat to wood. Although most of their damage occurs in living trees or in logs or lumber that is still green, a few occasionally invade furniture. Some may have laid eggs in the wood before it was constructed. Since most of the insects are wood borers, the damage is usually visible in the form of holes or exposed tunnels along a board's surface. Many people attribute character to old country furniture that has worm holes.

9

Other Buying Considerations

Investment and Resale

Although almost everyone agrees that old furniture prices will continue to rise, there are different degrees of optimism. Those who are bullish on the subject see old furniture as an *investment*, while those with a conservative outlook view it as only having *resale value*. Usually the investment view has been reserved for period antiques, mainly those with values in the thousands of dollars. Even though old furniture rarely gets into such a range, a fast rise in its prices during the boom has stirred up the notion that it, too, is a big profit venture. The great success of fad items like pie safes and claw-footed tables has promoted the extra optimism.

In contrast with the dramatic big gainers, the majority of old furniture belongs in a less speculative category. Its prices, while they are apt to rise, are fairly predictable. In general they will stay ahead of the economy, but a significant portion of any profit you might make may easily be erased by factors involved in liquidation, such as advertising costs, touch-up repairs, or a desire to sell too fast.

Old furniture, in the main, is more of a hedge against inflation, a hold-its-own kind of phenomenon. It has a very definite advantage of not depreciating like new furniture. Unlike new furniture, which generally will have gone down 50 percent or more in its first two years, old furniture is likely to increase and continue to rise as new furniture depreciates even further.

The current old furniture status is that it is still in demand at boom levels (not as high as during the height of the boom), but the supply has shrunk significantly. This situation tends to support higher prices, both retail and wholesale. Actually, while prices have not risen much above an inflationary level, some buyers, consumers and dealers alike, have been intimidated by the increases. Dealers have been reluctant to purchase furniture at higher levels because of a presumed greater risk. It is significant, however, that some dealers have reported that if they are willing to pay the price for higher-quality wholesale goods, they do not have the trouble finding buyers one would expect. As usual, they say, better-quality furniture is easier to sell.

Despite prices that are threatening to some, there are good indications that old furniture will hold its value. One of them is that prices have not gone down. Articles of old furniture, even the more ephemeral fad items, are not reflooding the market. Antique shops, furthermore, are not going out of business any more than they ever did, and offshoot venture like furniture repair and refinishing are still busy enough.

Predicting the future prices of established kinds of old furniture is easier than for the new varieties that will become popular in the next few years. The stability of golden oak, Victorian walnut, and all kinds of country furniture seems assured, but the pricing that will accompany the more distinctly twentieth-century styles is difficult to anticipate. Much of it, especially the massive and "traditional" styles, will be of poorer quality and will have less resale value. Because the woods and construction will often be inferior, more discrimination will be needed in choosing them. A poor piece will not hold its value, will present more repair problems (both now and later), and will often cost as much as something that can be found elsewhere that is considerably better. The newer old furniture should continue as at least a break-even proposition. There will be less to be made in profit but there will be a probable stability in a resale role.

Despite a less-than-investment status, there is enough money involved in old furniture to warrant a careful selection in buying it. A few extra minutes spent in comparisons can make a very significant added return when, for whatever practical reason, you finally decide to sell it. The following topics seem to be the main ones related to ensuring a good resale return. All of them are based on buying furniture in good condition at average prices. Some of the topics have been touched on earlier in various chapters. Some will have as much to do with buying for pleasure and use as for ensuring value:

age
fad popularity
functional considerations
handmade vs. factory
legitimacy of repairs
natural finish vs. stained
overall condition
scarcity
veneer vs. solid wood
wood quality

Scarcity

You would think that something that is rare or odd would be more valuable, but this isn't true with old furniture. Scarcity is important in some respects, but it is surprising how much demand there is for things that are fairly common. Many things that are familiar, rather than being considered trite, have a classic appeal and are considered safe by conservative shoppers. Many also find common, simple pieces easier to blend with their existing furniture. Rarity is more of a concern to collectors,

Pegged joints and scribe marks. Two signs of hand craftsmanship often found in old split-bottom chairs.

but don't rule it out if a piece has other desirable features. Just don't buy for rarity alone.

Age

Some museum pieces, if they are old enough, are valued solely for their age. With period furniture intended for home use, age is a necessary ingredient but is important to a lesser degree. With popular old furniture, age helps, but in individual pieces may be considerably outweighed by other desirable elements, especially style.

The only definite criterion regarding age in old furniture is that an article needs to have enough of it to separate it from used furniture.

Handmade vs. Factory

Something that is handmade has a big edge when it comes to resale value. In country furniture especially, pegged joints and scribe marks convey the extra skill involved in making handmade pieces and are impressive as signs of high precision in a world that had comparatively little technology.

They also represent a degree of patience many people today find amazing.

Although handmade furniture deserves distinction for its methods, there are other factors (state of repairs, for example) that need to be taken into account. With furniture that is to be lived with and enjoyed, any single consideration must be subordinate to a complex of others. Something that is handmade but poorly designed in terms of aesthetics or usefulness will have a limited market. Something lacking in overall quality and condition will appeal to only a small number of people.

Veneer vs. Solid

Some of the thin veneers that began to be used in the thirties have created a lot of prejudice against veneers in general. Although some veneer furniture that is to be found is extremely well constructed, there is an almost universal preference for solid wood. Selling points for good veneered furniture are its thickness and how long it has lasted if it is still intact.

Natural Finish vs. Stained

With the exception of eclectic parlor sets and arts and crafts/mission oak, very little furniture had been stained until just after World War I. The main use of stain that began then with combination furniture was on a far greater scale than ever before. The method of mixing stain with finish made it much more economical to apply, as well as allowing cheaper woods to be used. Huge amounts of both stylized reproductions and massive furniture were produced using the mixed finishing materials. The variation in quality in both types was great.

Well-made articles of combination furniture are likely to hold their value and even return a profit when bought economically. It is difficult to see how the cheaper items, being so much like today's poorer furniture, will ever amount to much. Items like smoking stands and Martha Washington sewing cabinets have succeeded, though, due to fad appealing characteristics.

Overall Condition

The better the shape something is in, naturally the better the price it will bring. Some wear is tolerated, especially in primitive country furniture, but extremes of it, or out-and-out damage, reduce values. Wear and damage are less accepted in more formal furniture. Some of the other considerations of overall condition include:

• working parts that function well
• presence of all parts, including hardware
• a finish that is intact and has some luster
• a satin (semi-gloss) finish, generally preferred for old furniture even though a gloss is usually more durable.

Wood Species and Quality

The preferred, but not necessarily most popular species are cherry, Honduras mahogany, and walnut. Other woods, because they are more affordable and still have some desirable features, also have a share of the investment spotlight. Oak, poplar, pine, and maple are the chief examples. Exact preferences vary from place to place and according to different tastes and pocketbooks. There may be some changes in the future as preferences are modified by a different set of available styles (older styles will be less obtainable, later ones more). Wood with a regular grain and texture will likely continue to be in greatest demand, all other things being equal.

Legitimacy of Repairs

This mainly has to do with the quality of repairs and the replacement of missing parts. The sophisticated buyer looks for restoration work that is not too noticeable and is sufficiently strong. Among the things he is likely to notice and care about are:

- parts missing or poorly replaced
- accuracy of veneer replacement
- appropriate color matching
- patina sanded away
- sufficiently thick drawer bottom replacements
- appropriate hardware
- jerry-rigged repairs

Functional Considerations

Functional considerations were not always in the mind of furniture makers. Tables and chairs were made too high or too low, chests with drawers too small, and cabinets with shelves too narrow. Not only were dimensions sometimes off, but obstacles were occasionally built in that prevented use of the furniture in the first place. There were drop-leaf tables without enough width for seating, table skirts too low for leg-room, and chairs with a variety of comfort problems. It is especially important to look for these things in examining country furniture, which was often less subject to a functional scrutiny than factory types.

Fad Popularity

If you can determine which kinds of furniture are going to be the phenomenal big sellers, you can think in terms of investment and not just resale value. The most common characteristic of today's fad items is some type of quaintness. All fad items—

pie safes, ice boxes, etc. are decidedly old-fashioned and have a remarkably distinct, sometimes "cute" character. Other characteristics found in some items are a high degree of decoration or ornament (gingerbread chair, brass beds) or a larger number of compartments (Hoosier cabinets, pigeonhole desks).

Reupholstery and Slipcovers

The aim of this section is to provide an overview of redoing old upholstery. Special attention will be given to its selection, some of the reupholstery steps that may be needed, the alternative of slipcovers, and some of the problems involved in getting the work done by an upholstery shop. Some perspective will also be given for doing the work yourself.

Although old articles of upholstered furniture are not as available as wooden ones, there is an occasional piece to be found that is both attractive and economical to renovate. There would be more, but their appearance, once enough places had become worn or damaged, was discouraging to their owners, and the usual resort became the trash dump or the woodpile.

Comfort

Even though books on upholstery seldom mention it, one of the first considerations in buying old upholstery needs to be comfort. Comfort has two aspects, the physical dimensions of a piece—its size and shape on the one hand, and its upholstery, the springs, padding, cushions, etc. on the other. The dimensional side of comfort is particularly important with older pieces. Many early items were made according to the notion of *sitting* rather than the more modern idea of *lounging*. The parlor set, in particular, was built for the more formal posture, and there were others with the same orientation. Most of them are used today for decoration more than for relaxing.

A consideration of size is important with *ladies' chairs*. Ladies' chairs were made in a variety of styles up until the thirties. They are not at all rare today and may tempt you several times if you shop for old upholstery. Their small proportions make them appealing, but they are not suited for larger individuals.

Another phenomenon to be found is the sofa that is too short for napping. Other kinds of discomfort related to size are more subtle. Some of the comfort factors that deserve scrutiny are seat height and depth and back slope. Ordinarily they are the main aspects of dimensional comfort.

Another part of upholstery that involves comfort is the arm support. In well-designed sofas and chairs, the arm rests are integrated with the back and seating to provide a natural arm support. Some are designed at the same time to provide a relaxing position for reading and handwork, those on chairs especially. Other sofas and chairs have arm rests that were seemingly tacked on after the main business of seating. Legs are other parts often made with an add-on character.

To be sure of an article's comfort, do some comparative sitting, enough of it to find out what better comfort is. One of the best ways to compare comfort is to visit a new furniture store having a variety of upholstered items. One of the worst times to try out upholstery, however, is when you are tired. You will think you're comfortable only because of your fatigue.

There are two general approaches to reupholstery, and each relates a little differently to comfort. With reupholstery itself, essentially a rebuilding process, comfort can be reengineered to some extent with new padding and cushions and a beefing-up of springs. With slipcovers, the second approach, economics and expedience are dominant motives, and a piece's comfort is usually taken more the way it comes. Despite the simpler nature of slipcovers, there is nothing wrong, of course, in first overhauling paddings and cushions. The changes can be far more simple than a complete upholstery.

Changes in dimensions, except for lowering or raising seat height, are seldom practical, either with slipcovers or reupholstery. The dimensional side of comfort, then, is seldom altered.

Evaluating Old Upholstery

In addition to ensuring comfort in what you buy, it is also necessary to assess an item's structure to determine how much reupholstery may be needed or if it qualifies as a slipcover candidate. Because they are covered, not all of the parts of an upholstered item can be examined directly. The frame and its joints are partly visible but also largely obscured.

Although some aspects of the frame and joints can be seen by turning the piece over and removing the thin material used to prevent dust accumulation, the main process needs to be one of applying pressure here and there on the outside and lifting corners. Loose or broken joints can usually be detected by a thorough process of manipulating a piece in this way. If any such joints are located, at least a partial dismantling is required and a gluing and clamping procedure needed to reconnect them. Frame repair can be a major and costly operation in reupholstery.

Some of the important parts of a piece's *seating* structure are in partial view after it is turned over and the dust cover removed. The parts that become visible are the *springs*, *ties*, and *webbing*. Several aspects need to be considered. Check the springs to see whether any are out of alignment, broken, or have gone up through the seat's padding. A spring that is out of alignment probably has one or more broken ties. The ties are part of the system of twine that connects adjacent springs to each other and each spring to the chair (or sofa) frame. Better upholstery has six- or eight-way ties; cheaper varieties, just four. The ones with four-way ties are the most likely to have problems.

The next thing to inspect is the webbing. (Not all pieces have it; some have steel-framed springs instead.) The webbing's function is to suspend the entire seating and give it cushioning. The springs are sewed or clipped to it and it is fastened to the frame. All of the fastening points where the webbing holds the springs should be secure and the webbing itself tight and free of dry rot.

A similar system of springs, ties, and webbing is to be found in the backs of some furniture. Most of the parlor sets, however, simply had webbing covered by padding materials. Because most backs are covered by upholstery fabric on both sides, their parts cannot be inspected like seating. The usual procedure to find out if a back is satisfactory is to feel it. A back that is sagging probably has broken or loose webbing. (The seating, too, can have this obvious symptom.) If the article is going to be taken apart and completely rebuilt anyway, it doesn't matter.

In going over an old piece, the two main things to check are whether there are any bare or bunched spots in the padding and how much buoyancy is left in the padding. Places that are uneven can often be straightened with a strong, thin, smoothly sharpened wire (called a *regulator*). A lack of buoyancy is a greater problem. It is caused by the compacting of padding, especially cotton, over years of use. Sometimes a hardened padding can be refluffed by hand, but the usual approach is to buy new materials since their cost is relatively low.

Cushions, if they have to be replaced, are usually a greater expense than padding. Better ones are carefully engineered for smooth contours and soft cushioning (some of them trap air in small pockets). Cheaper cushions are made of plain foam.

The largest variable in reupholstery costs is often the fabric, the final cover. Prices range very widely and you usually pay retail when you have something done by a professional shop. If you do have something done by an upholsterer, he should be able to advise you about the durability and color fastness of the fabric.

Slipcovers

The primary advantage of slipcovers is, of course, that they are cheaper—far cheaper than having a piece completely reupholstered. They are cheaper still if you can do the work yourself or find someone who does them at home. First you must decide whether the old upholstery is in good enough shape to be covered. (All the points of examination already mentioned apply.) A few minor repairs—some stuffing moved here and there, or an old tear sewn—and a piece can easily be kept in a slipcover category. You may want to go even further in doing repairs, but eventually a greater severity or number of problems will call for reupholstery measures.

In some sets of circumstances the condition of old upholstery might mean having to choose arbitrarily between slipcovers and the simple application of new upholstery fabric. Assuming that everything else is all right and you do the work yourself, applying new fabric often amounts to roughly the same difficulty. The old fabric can be taken off and its pieces used as patterns for the new covering. The complexity in the job is in the sewing and other fastening procedures. Making slipcovers requires special techniques, especially in measuring and making allowances. The fit of slipcovers must be accurate, but not too tight to prevent an ease of removal and replacement. They must, in fact, be loose enough to allow for any shrinkage that may occur in cleaning.

The Costs Involved

The money you spend with old upholstery can vary tremendously. If you buy selectively, you can save a lot; if you do the work yourself, you can save considerably more. If you pay too much for the piece to begin with; have the work done blindly, without getting an appropriate estimate; or spend too much on materials, particularly the final fabric, you will probably not thoroughly enjoy the finished piece.

Many old furniture dealers do not know the work that is involved in reupholstery. Many of them set their prices too high, thinking that practically all a piece needs is a new fabric. The fact is that prices paid for old upholstery should be very low, lower than for wooden furniture, which, by comparison, can be seen more for what it is. With dilapidated old pieces, all that you are paying for is a frame with reusable springs (probably), and the old fabric to be disas-

sembled and used for pattern pieces. In less run-down cases, even though there may be some salvageable cushions and padding, a piece is only worth more *theoretically*. It may still have hidden problems. You should pay more for only the sure-fire bets, the ones that have passed a scrupulous examination or the ones with highly compensating aesthetic merits.

If you are going to have work done by an upholsterer, the most important thing to do, after contacting one with a reputation for fairness and good work, is to establish a well-understood working agreement. Even conscientious shop owners can make mistakes or unconsciously take advantage when circumstances are ambiguous. With an appropriate agreement you will have at least an overview of the work to be done, an estimate of the total cost, and provisions for unforeseen work (such as hidden frame damage).

Although working agreements between customers and upholsterers are usually less spelled out, a *10 percent estimate* has become a recent popular arrangement. With it, an upholsterer finding unexpected work cannot exceed 10 percent of the agreed-on figure without the customer's O.K. The practice does provide protection but is not as certain as a specific price quote. Some shop owners, however, will not make quotes when there is a possibility of hidden work: they feel that too much of a gamble is involved. Successful upholsterers who customarily make quotes typically make them high enough to exceed anything unexpected.

Choosing an appropriate fabric for your piece can get difficult and expensive. If you have a zealous need for quality and a contrasting situation in your pocketbook, you will probably be disappointed several times as you leaf through an upholsterer's fabric sample books. The variety of samples both in terms of design and quality is usually staggering unless you've looked before and have a general idea of what you want. Something that by itself makes selection easier is the price and quality coding that generally accompanies each sample.

Finding an authentic fabric can be something of a problem, particularly if you do not have the old one to go by. One of the favorite fabrics on many of the Victorian parlor sets was *red plush*, a moderate-quality velvet. *Horsehair*, a slick type of black fabric, was another favorite. Both kinds of material are available through most upholstery shops. If your upholsterer does not know an authentic fabric for your piece, looking at some old Sears catalogs will give a good picture of the fabrics used in some time frames, especially the late Victorian and afterwards.

Upholstering something yourself can be enjoyable as well as a savings. The work is relatively clean and an appropriate challenge to someone with a few sewing skills, some patience, and the motivation to finish the work and do a good job. As far as acquiring specific skills, most of them can be learned from the selection of upholstery books in even small-town libraries. A short upholstery course, one with time to work on your own piece, will usually pay for itself several times over. If you live in a small town, the major drawback of doing your own work is that you may not have immediate access to all the upholstery supplies you may need. Most are available, however, through upholstery courses and through some fabric stores in larger towns and cities.

Trunks

An old trunk is a neat form of storage.

With its large depth and relatively tight lid seal, it makes an almost ideal blanket chest. Its antique woods and metals add something interesting to almost any style of room decoration. Many people, even those without an interest in old furniture, buy trunks for their singular good looks.

Although many trunks can be found in good usable condition, most need some amount of work to be attractive. For several reasons, especially an unavailability of authentic paper lining materials (any remaining old ones have decayed over the years), the work done to trunks has been more of a creative affair than a careful matter of restoring originality. New materials have been used for linings and new treatments (mainly paints) have been used for trunk outsides. Many people have had to do trunks in a slapdash way, however, because of not knowing where to get replacement parts or suggestions for decorating. Both are available from the following:

Antique Trunk Co.
3706 W. 169th St.
Cleveland, OH 44111

Charolette Ford Trunks, Ltd.
Box 536
302 E. 11th St.
Spearman, TX 79081

At least half the work of renovating most old trunks is putting in a new lining. One way to estimate the amount of work is to count the number of separate inside surfaces to be covered. Trunks with two or three lids and compartments have twice as many actual surfaces as a plain one.

There are two general approaches to lining trunks: Line the walls directly with some material; or make a cardboard pat-

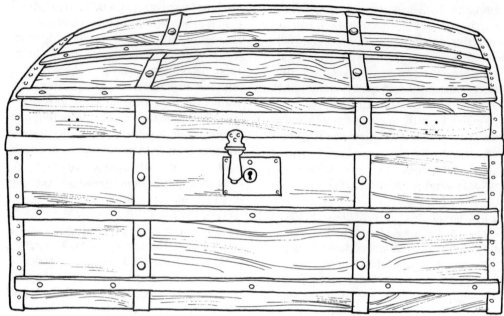

An old trunk. Hard to beat for charm and the storage of winter things.

tern for each surface, cover it with the material, then attach it to the walls.

Although almost any material may be used for lining, many people prefer a small print wallpaper or fabric with an early American flavor. Other materials include old newspapers coated with varnish, some of the newer pastable shelf papers, and sheet copper. There are many other possibilities that are suitable.

If using a fabric or paper, choose one that is thick enough to prevent the cardboard or the trunk's old lining from showing through. Generally it is not necessary to remove all of the old lining, just that which is loose. Water-thinned white glue applied with a brush makes a good adhesive.

Mirrors

Up through the middle ages all mirrors were simple pieces of polished metal and were highly prized because of their scarcity. Around 1500, craftsmen living in Venice developed processes for making mirrors of polished glass backed with a reflective coating of tin and mercury. Both the manufacture of the glass and the silvering process were secrets until a French diplomat lured some of the Venetian craftsmen to his own country.

Although the making of the glass alone improved several times in the following centuries, there was no basic change in the silvering process until 1840, when a solution containing real silver began to be used in place of the old ingredients. A factory process of making mirrors began shortly afterward and led to incorporating them into early Victorian furniture styles.

The entire Victorian period emphasized mirrors. They were almost always included in its bedroom furniture and were frequently designed into sideboards, hall-racks, and many kinds of cabinets. Most mirrors, probably the great majority, had beveled edges. Beveled-edge mirrors today have a considerable charm and charisma. They represent a richness of detail that began to disappear with the end of the Victorian styles.

A deteriorated silvering is a frequent problem with any type of old mirror. Sometimes the reflective layer is in poor enough condition to, at least supposedly, need stripping and resilvering. There are few places that do the work, however; most of them are located in large cities. If you live in or near a city, you may well be able to get a mirror redone reasonably. Someone living remote from a resilvering shop, on the other hand, my find that the crating and transportation costs for shipping his mirror both ways can make the price of resilvering exceed the amount involved in ordering a completely new mirror.

Many mirror owners, unless they have something that is very treasured or complex in shape, decide to get a new replacement if their old mirror glass has been scratched or otherwise damaged. Even small scratches, unless they are buffed away, show up visibly after resilvering. Buffing is often expensive.

Plain-edged mirrors can be bought and custom-cut at most glass shops. Beveled mirrors are mainly big city items but can usually be ordered in small towns through glass shops. Stock sizes like 16 by 24 inches or 18 by 30 inches are naturally the cheapest, but even an irregularly shaped mirror can often be custom-ordered by sending a pattern for it.

One of the most popular methods of dealing with a deteriorated beveled mirror is to scrape away the old silvering and install a new plain-edged mirror behind it.

Paint and varnish remover is sometimes helpful in the scraping process. Two problems that can occur, however, are an inability to remove all of the old silvering and the presence of scratches.

Hardware

Most old furniture has hardware. While just about all types have a working function, some devices also play a large part in an individual piece's attractiveness and are a good indicator of its style. Hardware, whenever possible, needs to be as authentic as possible, but the cost can be surprisingly high if many replacements are needed. Parts, such as hinges, that are strictly functional, need to be in good working order to do their job and provide smooth functioning.

Drawer Pulls

A single pull usually consists of a *bale* (the handle part) and a *backplate* (used for decoration and protecting the surrounding wood). Most drawer pulls were made in some form of brass. A few varieties on cheaper furniture were made with *stamped* brass backplates and bales made of *steel*. The better ones were made entirely of *cast* brass: they were thicker and had more detail. Several mail-order companies sell brass pulls. Some sell a variety; others specialize in types made mostly for golden oak. (See the list at the end of this section.) Brass pulls tend to get expensive, when, at 4 or 5 dollars apiece (1983 prices), several drawers need to have one pair each plus, perhaps, escutcheons.

Escutcheons

The kind of escutcheons generally asso-

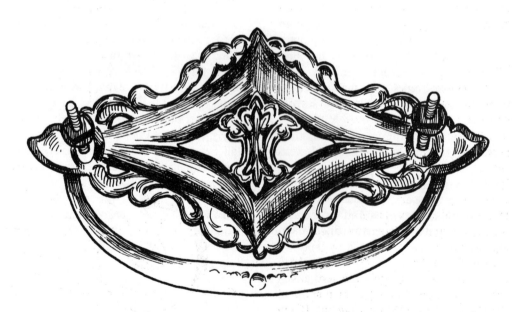

Cheaper brass pulls were made of stamped metal. Note the front and back views.

A keyhole escutcheon of a type found on Eastlake furniture.

with a piece, it is wise to pry out the sockets to prevent them scratching your floor. (Save everything in case you decide later that casters are useful and can be tolerated.) Casters have a significant bearing on furniture height; tables are particularly affected. When practicality dictates a change in table height or the casters you have are not desirable, special leg height adjusters can be purchased from some of the companies. They are not especially attractive, however.

ciated with furniture are the ones that surround and decorate keyholes. Keyhole escutcheons were usually made of wood or brass. The wooden ones were sometimes used on country pieces, but more often on factory furniture made of walnut or chestnut. Brass escutcheons were used more on factory pieces alone. A limited variety of escutcheons are available through mail order.

Casters

Casters were one of the practical aspects of several kinds of furniture. Some early period types had casters made either completely of brass or with brass bodies and porcelain rollers. The ordinary factory casters that began to be used late in the Victorian era first had wooden rollers, then Bakelite plastic. Replacements for the factory kinds are available at many hardware stores and through some of the catalogs listed later.

Most factory casters consist of a *wheel*, a *stem* that goes up into the leg, and a *socket* that holds the stem in place and prevents the wood from wearing out. If you do not want to use the casters that come

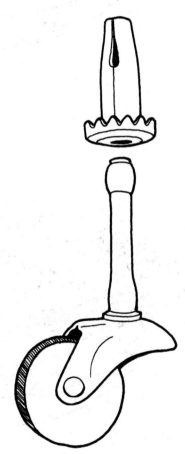

A factory-made caster with its socket.

Mushrooms knobs similar to this one in shape were used on most kinds of country furniture.

Knobs

Although knobs are generally regarded as being handles for doors, on country furniture they were used for drawers also. The main type of knob used with country furniture was the mushroom knob, a kind that varied considerably in its design. Almost all of them were designed at the discretion of individual craftsmen, and a single knob can rarely be matched by those available at hardware stores or through the mail. There are two alternatives for replacing missing knobs: Either have duplicates made by someone with a lathe, or buy a whole set of new replacements. With either alternative, color matching is a big problem, sometimes even when using the same species of wood. Old wood is different in color from new wood and staining or bleaching is usually needed. Knobs made of glass or porcelain are available at some hardware stores and through catalog sales. Although they are not as authentic (in their day they were usually sold as replacements for wooden ones), they do avoid the color-matching problem.

Latches and Catches

Latches and catches were used on cabinet doors to keep them closed and to make them align properly. The most common type of latch was the *block* and *screw latch* discussed under "Furniture with Doors" in chapter 6. Another type of latch was generally fastened to the inside of a door. It closed by having one edge rotate into a groove cut in one of the cabinet's shelves. The most frequent type of country furniture device was the *hook* and *eyelet catch* connecting the inside of a door with one of the shelves. It was often a solution for doors that had been warped out of position.

Factory furniture, although it began by using simple wooden devices, after a time turned to more sophisticated things for latching and catching. Finer furniture often employed *cupboard turn knobs*, which could be rotated to open and closed positions. Other devices, of which there were dozens of types made, had internal springs.

Replacing country wooden latches or catches means either having them made or finding substitutes. Matching replacements for some of the factory spring catches are

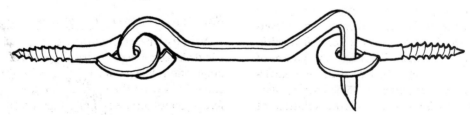

A hook and eyelet catch. Used for holding in place a door not held by a latch. Usually worked from inside.

available, but others will rarely be found, even through informal sources.

Hinges

Hinges that work well are vital to the proper functioning of doors. Hinges that are too thin for the job often become bent and allow a door to get out of alignment. Although they can often be replaced by thicker hinges, new cuts into the wood with a chisel are needed to accommodate the extra thickness. One of the biggest problems with old hinges is removing their screws. Often the difficulty is due to their accumulating rust over the years. A stuck screw may need the force of a hammer applied to the top of a screw driver that is held with a turning tension on the screw.

Sometimes the screw slot may have been damaged. A hacksaw blade can sometimes be used to saw a deeper slot. Often a longer screw is needed to replace one that has grown loose because of poor installation. Many sizes of hinges in both steel and solid brass are available at most hardware stores. If you buy packaged hinges be sure the screws that are included are strong enough to be turned tight. Avoid brass *plated* hinges. They are not much cheaper and the brass tends to flake off after a period of time.

Cleaning Brass Hardware

Some brass needs more cleaning than other brass. Basically there are three levels of deterioration—*corrosion*, *full tarnish*, and *light tarnish*. There are three groups of remedies; each is better suited for a particular level, but there is some overlap also:

Corrosion—A *15 percent* solution of sulfuric acid removes corrosion and full tar-

A "pigeon" latch, popular after 1900. It was an improvement because of its internal spring.

nish fast. It also eats holes in clothing and burns skin. Safety glasses and acid-resistant rubber gloves need to be worn, and the solution must be used carefully. It is applied with fine to medium steel wool.

Full tarnish—There are three home formulas, all much safer than sulfuric acid but also requiring more work: (1) straight household ammonia and fine steel wool; (2) lemon juice, salt, and fine steel wool; and (3) vinegar, salt, and fine steel wool.

Light tarnish and polishing—A brass polish such as Brasso is used with a cloth or soft paper.

Professional metal refinishing shops use a sequence of different cleaning and polishing compounds in conjunction with a buffing wheel. Their methods are superior, but are, of course, more expensive.

Removing Rust from Iron or Steel

A rotary wire brush attached to an electric drill seems to work better than liquid preparations like naval jelly. Rotary brushes come in two or three grades to suit different job roughnesses. Large ones are also made to fit electric bench wheels. Things

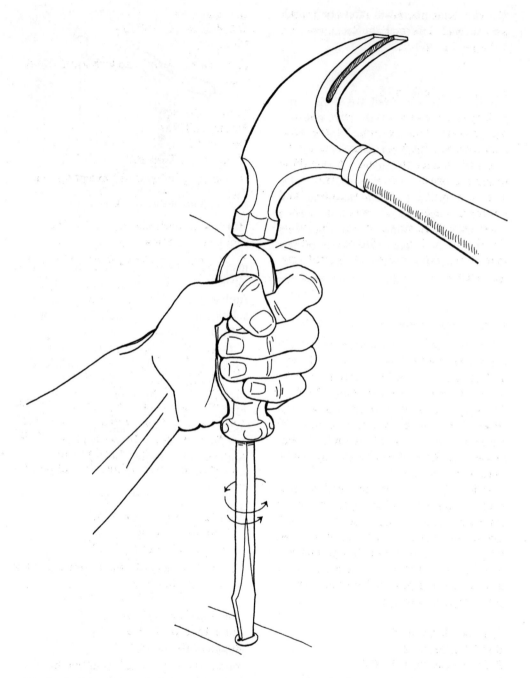

Striking the screwdriver with a hammer while exerting counterclockwise pressure is a good way to loosen a stuck screw. The hammer blow does most of the work, especially if there is rust.

like iron beds can be worked on directly with the drill. Smaller items like hinges need to be held in a vise.

Stripping Pie Safe Tins

Stripping pie safe tins of paint can be a big problem, because most of the ordinary tools you might use (wire brush, steel wool) will scratch the surface. A safe thing to use is a brush made with *brass* bristles. They are available in many grocery and hardware stores as pot scrubbers. Brass does not scratch several metals, including tin. With pie safe tins it also has the advantage of bringing out the metal's aged grayish green luster.

Hardware Supplies

The suppliers in this section mainly sell decorative hardware—pulls, escutcheons, and the like. Functional hardware will be included under "General Suppliers" below. The suppliers listed all work through mail order. Even though many of the companies have been in business a long time, it is impossible to know for sure exactly which ones will continue.

It is suggested that you send a prospective supplier a note together with a stamped, self-addressed post card and ask that he send you a catalog, or if he cannot, reply with the post card telling you its cost or other circumstances. If he is no longer in business, the post office should return your original envelope.

Antique Hardware Co.
Box 877, Dept. 12
Redondo Beach, CA 90277
Specializes in golden oak and related hardware.

Ball and Ball
463 W. Lincoln Highway
Exton, PA 19341
Specializes in period and architectural hardware.

Horton Brasses
Nooks Hill Rd.
Box 95 AT
Cromwell, CT 06416
A wide range of hardware except for golden oak.

Ritter & Son Hardware
Gualala, CA 95445
Golden oak and related, some ice box hardware.

General Suppliers

Albert Constantine and Son
2050 Eastchester Road
Bronx, NY 10461
Offers a very wide range of veneers plus finishing supplies, lumber and moldings, caning materials, upholstery supplies, hand tools, decoration and functional hardware, Chairloc, leg height adjusters, table slides, etc.

Woodcraft Supply Corp.
313 Montvale Avenue
Woburn, MA 01888
Very wide variety of general woodworking tools, some hardware.

The Woodworker's Store
21801 Industrial Blvd.
Rogers, MN 55374
About the same as Constantine but with less emphasis on veneers and a wider selection of functional hardware.

Index